BIKING

GLA

Clyde Vall

C000031257

RICHARD PEACE is a freelance teacher and writer. He was educated at Queen Elizabeth Grammar School, Wakefield and Magdalen College, Oxford, obtaining a degree in Modern History.

He lives in Wakefield, West Yorkshire and when not cycling or walking in Britain he travels and teaches abroad.

ALSO BY RICHARD PEACE

- YORKSHIRE DALES CYCLE WAY
- WEST YORKSHIRE CYCLE WAY
- MOUNTAIN BIKING - WEST & SOUTH YORKSHIRE
(all Hillside Guides)
- THE MACLEHOSE TRAIL (HONG KONG)

A full list of current Hillside guides can be found at the end of the book

BIKING COUNTRY

GLASGOW

Clyde Valley & Loch Lomond

Richard Peace

HILLSIDE

HILLSIDE
PUBLICATIONS
11 Nessfield Grove
Keighley
West Yorkshire
BD22 6NU

First published 1996

© Richard Peace 1996

ISBN 1 870141 45 8

Cover illustrations:
Top - Mugdock Country Park
Bottom - Strathclyde Loch
Back cover: The Clyde from Erskine Bridge;
Kvaerner Shipyard; Bowling Basin
(Richard Peace/Big Country Picture Library)

Page One:
Looking over Loch Lomond from Garadhban Forest

Printed in Great Britain by
Carnmor Print and Design
95-97 London Road
Preston
Lancashire
PR1 4BA

CONTENTS

INTRODUCTION

The majority of rides in this guide can be reached from Glasgow within 40 minutes road travel and most are within cycling distance of a train station. It is ideal for residents of the area covered or for tourists visiting the delights of Glasgow and surrounding area.

Geography

The cityscape of Glasgow, with a surprising number of green spots and country parks, is complemented by often surprisingly little-explored surrounding areas including the Campsie Fells, the Strathblane valley bordering their western edge and the hills round the Firth of Clyde. The southern shores of Loch Lomond are the furthest north ventured within these pages; the area popularly known as the Trossachs really needs a more northerly base to be properly appreciated.

To the west the towns of Dumbarton, Greenock and Port Glasgow straddle the Clyde. Once centres of heavy industry, most notably shipbuilding, these towns now suffer more than their fair share of urban blight, but viewed by bike from the rising moors above them you are privileged to a unique blend of unusual dockside scenery aside the stretching mouth of the Clyde as it meets the sea, all backed by rising hills. To the east the once prominent iron and steel industry in Coatbridge and Airdrie has melted away but there are still plenty of green fingers of countryside in the suburbs bordering the Clyde.

The Human Landscape

Originally centred on heavy industry and especially shipbuilding in the past (fuelled by local deposits of iron ore, limestone and coal) Glasgow has followed the pattern of heavy industrial decline and service industry growth and, perhaps contrary to popular perception of it as a depressed northern city, it was European City of Culture in 1990 and is bidding to be a city of Architecture and Design in 1999 (to include a festival of architecture and design, a Millennium Tower and new galleries of Modern and Scottish Art). The ride round central Glasgow gives just a small taste of the huge number of museums and galleries, private and public, available here; well over 40!

Traditionally grazed by cattle and sheep many of the remoter areas away from the city have a very sparse population density, and tranquillity is but a short ride out of Glasgow's centre. On the moors south of Greenock or around the Campsie Fells one could be a hundred miles from Glasgow.

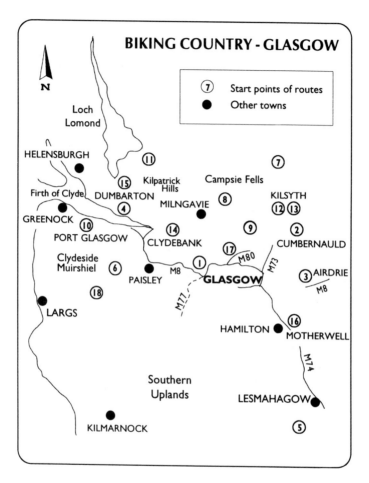

A profusion of castles are evidence of Scotland's long history of conquest and struggle. Scots, Picts, Vikings, Normans, Romans and English, Scottish and French monarchs have all at some time in the past battled to conquer the wildness of this land. Routes visit such monuments as the Roman Antonine Wall and Mugdock Castle, once home to historically influential nobility.

Weather

Late May or early June is said to be the best time to visit this area of comparatively heavy rainfall; annual averages range from a very reasonable 30-40 inches around Glasgow itself to a wet average of over 60 inches north of Loch Lomond and in some coastal areas further south. Summers are generally mild, if wet, but always watch out for sudden changes in the weather, especially on high ground. Any winter expedition even to the moderate higher altitudes described here should not be attempted by the inexperienced or taken lightly; follow the safety advice overleaf.

Gradient

The routes are graded by gradient steepness with additional specific comments on track surface:-

1 Mainly flat or with gentle slopes. Ideal for beginners or families.

2 Suitable for those with some experience wishing to build up more and to increase stamina. Requires a reasonable level of fitness. There may be the occasional steep gradient or extended moderate ones.

3 A real test. Only for more confident riders with a good level of fitness who like a challenge.

Owing to the nature of the countryside the surface of the tracks or paths may need some skill to negotiate. Grades may be mixed to describe various sections of a route so as to give an accurate picture of what it requires from the rider.

Bell's Bridge on the Clyde

EQUIPMENT

Clearly the most important piece of equipment is a bike that you can ride comfortably and safely. All the routes in this guide are suitable for mountain bikes and many for just about any kind of bike. The section on track surface in each route's introductory details should give you a good idea of whether a route is suitable for your particular bike. You should know how to do basic maintenance and carry the following basic tools, suitable for the jobs described. Because of the rougher conditions of off-road biking compared to road riding more maintenance is bound to be required on harder routes:

• *Puncture repair kit, spare inner tubes, air pump* - for burst inner tubes
• *Tyre levers* - for burst inner tubes
• *Range of spanners* - changing of wheels if not quick release; other common adjustments e.g. if pedal becomes loose
• *Small screwdriver* - adjusting gear mechanisms
• *Adjustable spanner* - will fit a number of nuts on the bike if they work loose.
• *Allen keys* - to fit various adjustments: handlebar stem, seat post etc.
• *Chainsplitter* - this tool not only takes chains apart but you may be able to rejoin your chain if it breaks whilst riding.

Keep moving parts, especially the chain, well lubricated. For a complete guide to maintenance see *The Bike Book* (Haynes).

A helmet should always be worn and I found the most other useful clothes items to be:-
• Padded shorts or three-quarter length bottoms depending on the weather.
• Durable footwear with a chunky sole to grip the pedal. Some pedal systems have clips or the facility to 'screw' the underneath of a sole to the pedal which can be useful to keep your feet on the pedals over rough ground. Practice disengaging your feet quickly from the system so you can use it safely.
• Good waterproof, breathable tops and bottoms.
• 'Fingerless' cycling gloves.

You heat up quickly on a bike so you should have the capability to take off and add a couple of layers of clothing and keep dry spares in bike bags or a small backpack. Too much weight or too large a backpack will destabilise you.

RIDING TECHNIQUE

If you are a beginner the first thing you may notice is that riding off road up any kind of gradient is immediately more difficult than road riding, because of the greater friction between tyres and surface. This effect varies according to the nature of the surface. Don't worry; take it easy and enjoy the scenery. For me the great joy of off road cycling is being able to go places and see things road cycling doesn't allow you to do.

Steep downhill sections require very close brake control. If you let them off for more than a second or two you can be seriously out of control. Don't try to force the bike where you think it ought to go; it will often run its own course if you concentrate on avoiding major obstacles. Relax your upper body and guide the bike; if you keep a very tight grip, hitting a small obstacle such as a stone is more likely to throw you off course.

On very steep uphill sections you may be able to cut across the track or road, if it is wide enough, in a zigzag pattern. You can start to do this if you think you will have to stop pedalling if you are heading straight up the hill. It effectively lessens your gradient and means you can take the climb in a more leisurely way. Obviously this is not a suitable technique for any main road sections. Following these tips should mean that after a time riding over varying terrain becomes almost second nature.

Please keep to the tracks and ride under control and at sensible speed downhill. Off road biking has gained a bad name with other countryside users because of the actions of a few irresponsible riders. There have even been calls from certain quarters for legislation to ban 'mountain' biking. To my mind 'mountain' biking is a misnomer as it implies the bikes can only be used on steep gradients and that you will be able to whizz up steep inclines without any effort whatsoever! Rather than a form of bicycle motorcross it should be viewed as a great way to keep fit and enjoy the countryside at the same time, as well as being exhilarating.

RIGHTS OF WAY AND COUNTRYSIDE BEHAVIOUR

In England many clear rights of way for walkers and cyclists exist; off-road cyclists are generally allowed on bridleways only (not footpaths) and such rights of way are usually clearly recorded on a definitive map. Walkers, cyclists and vehicles are allowed on byways. This system was not applied to Scotland under the relevant parliamentary statute and consequently the situation is a little more confused. There is no legal requirement for a definitive map of public rights of way to be kept by local authorities. Public rights of way in Scotland are simply defined using the following criteria:

1. The track must run from one public place to another, eg road, church
2. It must follow a more or less defined route
3. It must have been used openly and peaceably by members of the public otherwise than with the permission of the landowner, express or implied
4. It must have been so used without substantial and effective interruption for a period of twenty years or more

There is no definite answer as to whether cycles are allowed on public rights of way but there is a general tolerance of open access to the countryside *as long as it is used sensibly and respects landowners' wishes.* This general tolerance has led to the mistaken belief that there is no law of trespass in Scotland and people can go anywhere. This is certainly not so!

Because the legal position has long been ambiguous access for cycles on many rights of way may be difficult. Although the rights of way were chosen because they avoided numerous obstacles to cycles, these do still exist and you will have to get used to lifting your bike. Landowners are probably justified in erecting these as long as the way is passable to pedestrians (through the use of stiles etc).

The Scottish Rights of Way Society advise cyclists to use paths that 'appear to them to be appropriate, but to be prepared for the fact that they might be stopped, and that, if so, they probably have no legal recourse.' I have cycled all routes here and encountered no problems but if challenged by a landowner please accept the fact that you may not have a right of way and respect their wishes. As most of the off road sections are relatively short you might offer to push your bike to get to the next road/Sustrans route. Inclusion of a track in this book is not evidence of a right of way for bikes over it.

Designated cycle routes in Scotland

•*Sustrans* is short for sustainable transport. This charitable body has constructed a large number of linear routes. They are usually flat and of excellent quality surface. The organisation has already spent millions constructing these routes which are dedicated for walkers, cyclists or horses (or a combination of all three). Some of the routes in this guide take advantage of sections of Sustrans' paths. They are especially suitable for beginners or older and younger riders and are the easiest off road riding you will find.

At the time of writing Sustrans routes in the area are as follows, though they are constantly being updated and a number are under construction:

* Glasgow-Loch Lomond-Aberfoyle
* Paisley to Irvine and Ardrossan
* Johnstone to Greenock
* Airdrie to Bathgate
* Glasgow to Edinburgh (under construction)

•*District and regional councils* have also introduced designated cycle routes which may be specially constructed (e.g. the excellent Strathkelvin Railway Walkway), or may utilise minor roads, parks and cycle lanes through city centres, (e.g. Strathclyde's Glasgow to Paisley route). In the latter case you should be aware of the signs set out on page 18 for cyclists and motorists. Even then such routes can twist and turn and signs may be ambiguous at junctions.

•*British Waterways* usually allow cycling on suitable sections of towpath but do insist on you obtaining a permit. To use the sections contained in the routes in this book you can obtain a free permit from British Waterways. Canalside rides are only really suitable for youngsters under close supervision as the edges to the canal are not guarded.

Scotland's tracks through history

The *nature* of the country's tracks in many ways reflects the history of Scotland. The oldest tracks existing may be medieval or Roman though few of these come within our chosen area; they are usually found further south. In the 1700s cattle markets were held all over Scotland and were one of the country's economic mainstays. The cattle were often driven hundreds of miles over drove roads, often to be sold to English buyers. 'Kirk' and 'coffin' roads reflect the central role of religion in the lives of highlanders in centuries past. They were used to get to church or bring the bodies of the dead for burial, again often over considerable distances.

The English made their presence felt in the mid-eighteenth century with garrisons and military roads under General Wade. These were a reaction to Bonnie Prince Charlie's attempt to seize the English throne which was finally crushed at Culloden in 1746. These were added to by turnpike roads (toll roads) then roads built by public bodies, bringing us up to the present day. Tracks used may be one of the above type but their main use may now have been superseded by social and economic change and the coming of more modern roads. Sustrans paths most commonly follow disused railways, not hard to find in the post-Beeching era.

Much of Scotland outside the more 'touristy' areas is a clean, desolate and beautiful natural enviroment; please help to keep it that way by following the code overleaf.

At Dumbarton Castle

SCOTLAND: OFF-ROAD CYCLING - A CODE OF CONDUCT

Published in full with advisory introduction. Further copies available in the form of plastic handlebar tags from CTC and bike hire outlets.

With the advent of the mountain or all terrain bike more people are cycling off road, away from busy public roads. Off road cycling can be fun but it has its own hazards, and brings obligations to respect the interests of land managers and owners and to show courtesy to other recreations. This code gives basic advice on access to land in Scotland, on safety and on maintaining goodwill with other countryside users.

Access

Access to land has long been conducted as a matter of courtesy, tolerance and goodwill. However there is no legal right of access to land except on a right of way or where access has been specially negotiated. By law, the off-road cyclist is entitled to use cycle tracks and those public rights of way where a right to cycle exists under common law. It is not clear whether there is a right to cycle on pedestrian rights of way. There are permissive routes (as provided by bodies like the Forestry Commission) and many private and public companies do allow access to cyclists. Many of the traditional tracks through the glens will have right of way status for cycles, where use by cyclists has continued over the years, and where the route meets the other tests for a right of way.

Always be considerate and courteous when taking access and ask when in doubt.

THE CODE
- Think about others
- Cycle with consideration for others, always giving way to walkers and horse riders, and to farm and forest workers
- Give a friendly greeting to people you meet and acknowledge the courtesy of those who give way for you
- Watch your speed when close to others
- Try to avoid places heavily used by pedestrians, especially family groups. Always walk through congested areas. Do not alarm walkers by coming up silently behind them.
- Respect other land management activities, e.g. do not pass close to forestry operations until told it is safe to pass, or disturb sheep gathering or game shooting
- Follow the country code

14

Take Care of the Environment
- Keep to paths and hard tracks avoiding short cuts.
- Walk over very soft ground to avoid cutting it up.
- Avoid fierce braking and skids on downhill riding to minimise damage to path surfaces.
- Do not take bikes onto mountain tops and plateaux where vegetation is easily damaged.
- Leave no impact in remote areas. In particular take all litter home.
- Take special care when cycling downhill - this is when most accidents occur. Watch your speed on loose surfaces.
- Upland Scotland can be rough and remote. Cycle within your abilities as an accident or breakdown in a remote place could be serious.

UNDERSTAND THE BASICS OF MOUNTAIN SAFETY
- Take a companion in remote areas
- Remember crossing burns and rivers in spate can be dangerous
- Take a map and compass and know how to navigate
- Carry warm and waterproof clothing, emergency food, lamp, tools
- Consider wearing a helmet and protective clothing

YOUR BIKE SHOULD BE LEGAL FOR USE ON THE ROAD. DO NOT ARRANGE COMPETITIONS WITHOUT THE CONSENT OF THE LANDOWNER OR THE GUIDANCE OF THE SCOTTISH CYCLISTS UNION. SEEK CONSENT FOR RALLIES OR LARGE GROUPS.

OTHER INFORMATION

- Cyclists must adhere to the Highway Code
- A detailed map is recommended for more adventurous trips

THE COUNTRY CODE

- Enjoy the countryside and respect its life and work
- Guard against all risk of fire
- Fasten all gates
- Keep dogs under close control
- Keep to rights of way across farmland
- Use gates and stiles to cross fences, hedges and walls
- Leave livestock, crops and machinery alone.
- Take your litter home
- Help to keep all water clean
- Protect wildlife, plants and trees
- Take special care of country roads
- Make no unnecessary noise

SAFETY

- Ensure that your bike is safe to ride and prepared for all emergencies

- You are required by law to display working lights after dark on public highways (front and rear)

- Always carry some form of identification

- Always tell someone where you are going

- Learn to apply the basic principles of first aid

- Reflective materials on your clothes or bike can save your life (*obviously this applies doubly to road sections*)

- For safety on mountains refer to *Safety on Mountains,* a British Mountaineering Council publication

- Ride under control when going downhill, since this is often when serious accidents occur

- If you intend to ride fast off road it is advisable to wear a helmet. (*I recommend it on all routes at all times*)

- Particular care should be taken on unstable or wet surfaces

- In areas forested commercially there are special safety reasons for **not** passing through areas being worked on unless indicated to do so. Felling of trees in particular involves use of steel wire which can puncture tyres and may 'snap tight' if the winchman does not know you are there, causing fatal injuries.

ACCESS BY RAIL

There are various rules regarding the carrying of cycles on trains, depending on route, time and type of train! It would be a good idea therefore to get hold of the British Rail booklet *Cycling by Train*. It is available at most stations free of charge, and covers Regional Railways. It is likely the current situation will continue, with longer distance trips requiring a reservation and a £3 fee, and shorter routes within regional transport executive areas being generally free and on a 'first come, first served' basis, subject to peak hour restrictions. Because of the numerous rules and frequent changes, particularly in the current rail 'climate', the best idea is to ring the particular station you wish to use, or the nearest main station.

ABBREVIATIONS & SYMBOLS

Route descriptions
R - turn or bear right   **L** - turn or bear left   **¶** - signpost

Sketch maps

S - starting point of route

•••° - route (arrows indicate direction)   ⁄ - roads

⬦⁚ - route on roads   ⁄⁻˜ - other relevant tracks

⬤ - town/village   ⬤ - loch/reservoir   ༂༂ - woodland

⤳ - river   ⌒⌒⌒ - canal   +++++ - railway

The correct Landranger map is given together with six figure grid reference for the starting point and any additional maps available such as Sustrans leaflets. The maps included with the route descriptions might suffice as many of the routes are straightforward but do take an Ordnance Survey map and compass, especially on the more complex routes or when going through forest; they can put you back on the right track should you take a wrong turning. Route distances are given to the nearest kilometre or quarter mile.

Airdrie-Bathgate cycle path

CYCLING SIGNS

White on blue background

 Route recommended for pedal cyclists

 Direction of recommended cycle route

 Seen at crossing with pedestrian or road route

Route to be used by pedal cycles only

Segregated shared route for cyclists and pedestrians

Unsegregated shared route for cyclists and pedestrians

Bus and cycle lanes

White painted sign on road indicates cycle lane

Red border, white background

Pedal cycling prohibited

Caution, cycle route ahead (applicable to motorists)

SOME USEFUL ADDRESSES

Sustrans
35 King Street, Bristol BS1 4DZ
Tel. 0117-9268893

Cyclists' Touring Club
Cotterell House, 69 Meadrow, Godalming, Surrey GU7 3HS
Tel. 01483-417217

British Cycling Federation
National Cycling Centre, Stuart Street, Manchester M11 4DQ
Tel. 0161-2302301

Glasgow Tourist Information Centre
35 St. Vincent Place, Glasgow G1 2ER
Tel. 0141-2044400   (accommodation details)

The Scottish Rights of Way Society
John Cotton Business Centre, 10 Sunnyside, Edinburgh EH7 5RA
Tel. 0131-6522937

British Waterways
Canal House, Applecross Street, Glasgow G4 9SP
Tel. 0141-3326936

The Campsie Fells from near Gartness

CENTRAL GLASGOW

START Kelvingrove   **Grid ref.** 572662

DISTANCE 23km/14½ miles   **GRADIENT DIFFICULTY** 1

TIME ALLOWED The route itself is about three hours but you could easily turn it into an all day trip with the numerous museums and other attractions. If you have more time and want to take things more leisurely the two legs could be done on two separate trips.

TRACK SURFACE A mixture of tarmac Sustrans route, park tracks and minor roads. A few busy roads to cross and some co-use with pedestrians.

ORDNANCE SURVEY MAP Landranger 64, Glasgow
A suitable street atlas will give you useful detail. Sustrans leaflet - 'Glasgow-Loch Lomond Cycleway' (the blue one with detailed sectional maps from city centre to Balloch). For spur 'b' the Glasgow -Paisley guide is free from Strathclyde Roads (0141-2272581).

ACCESS Start from the Art Gallery and Museum. This lies just to the west of the M8 as it bends 90 degrees south to cross the Clyde (take Charing Cross exit). **Car** free parking outside Kelvingrove Museum and Art Gallery or by the entrance to Kelvin Hall Transport Museum (this may be full if an event is in progress at the neighbouring sports centre). **Train** The central area covered is ringed by Partick and Exhibition Centre train stations, either of which can be used as starting points.

SUMMARY
Easy cycling combines with some of the sights west of the centre of Glasgow. The Sustrans route from Glasgow to Loch Lomond and the Glasgow-Paisley cycle route combine to form two linear 'spines' radiating outward from the Kelvingrove cultural heart of Glasgow.

20

Museums, shipyards and leafy parks south of the river make this one of the most varied yet easiest rides for tourists wanting to discover the city's central attractions, or for locals wanting a different perspective on familiar features of their cityscape.

There shouldn't be any obstructions or difficulties as this is one of the easiest rides in the book. Allow plenty of time to explore the features along the way and remember to take a lock as you will want to leave your bike unattended to visit in detail the features on the route! Glasgow centre may not be solid with antique and atmospheric buildings as are some parts of Edinburgh or Stirling but the main features of this route are the numerous museums and galleries of the centre, together with a chance to sample the atmospheric scale of the Clydeside docks that can now only echo their former glory.

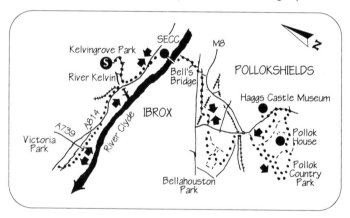

The Loch Lomond Cycleway spur

S Start at the parking area outside the museum and art gallery on the south bank of the river Kelvin in the Kelvingrove Park. From in front of this lovely building head west on the park track to meet Dumbarton Road facing the Kelvin Hall. Cross over the road with Partick Bridge on the right and go down Bunhouse Road on the marked green cycleway, with the entrance to the transport museum on your left. Coming to the junction with Old Dumbarton Road go **R** and follow the marked cycleway down and across the road. The road bears **L** after going past the back of a hospital and the entrance to Yorkhill Park on the left. Come to the end of the minor road and under the railway bridge and **R** onto the Sustrans Glasgow-Loch Lomond cycleway.

Cross over the bridge at the river Kelvin. Follow signs for the cycleway (don't be confused by signs leading you under a subway to Partick train station - the sign only indicates an access point). You will be guided **L** under the Expressway just after Partick fire station to climb very gently past a huge brick building, Meadowside Granary, attached to the Clydeside Port Authority building. Further up through the trees you may be able to see something currently under construction at the Kvaerner shipyard on the opposite bank, from where you can get an idea of the huge scale of shipbuilding operations.

Continue on the cycleway until you see three duckets (corrugated metal pigeon lofts) then on the **R** exit the cycleway on a path towards St. Pauls school which you can also see on the right. Keep **R** along Primrose Street with its typical Glasgow tenements. On hitting Dumbarton Road go **R** then immediate **L** by a bowling green, up Westland Drive. After about 100 yards on coming to traffic lights Victoria Park is opposite on the **R**. Fossil Grove museum is ¶ once in the park. From Fossil Grove you can retrace your steps back to the art gallery or continue on to the southern spur of the ride.

The Glasgow to Paisley spur

The Glasgow-Paisley cycle route starts at Bell's Bridge over the Clyde in the heart of Glasgow. If you are continuing on from the Loch Lomond section retrace your steps from Fossil Park and after recrossing the Kelvin ignore the left at the roundabout under the railway bridge back to your start point. Instead carry straight on, on the Loch Lomond Cycleway (if accessing from Kelvingrove simply turn **L,** not right, coming under the railway bridge after the section at the back of Yorkhill Park). Continue sandwiched between the railway on the left and the Clyde Expressway on the right until you meet a footbridge on the right.

Dismount to go over the bridge (and stay so until you have crossed Bell's Bridge). You find yourself at a small roundabout actually between Yorkhill and Stobcross quays on the other side of the bridge. Look for the Clyde walkway sign (blue fish on yellow background) on the other side of the roundabout roughly opposite the Customs House building on the right. Pass by the helipad and follow the quayside path by the Moat House International Hotel, which serves the adjoining Scottish Exhibition and Conference Centre. On the right is the futuristic looking Bell's Bridge. From both sides of the bridge you can see the Finniston Crane and north and south rotundas (circular brick constructions).

Having crossed the bridge follow the tarmac path to a T-junction and go **L**. From here the cycleway uses a combination of road and mixed pedestrian ways so pay attention to the signs (see page 18 for an explanation). Also many of the junctions have cycleway ¶. Go immediate **R** and follow Govan Road opposite the red brick structure on the left, heading south east past Festival Park on the right. Pick up a ¶ for the cycleway on the **L** to a crossroads with Brand Street at the Festival bar and go **R**. Shortly go **L** onto Cessnock Street and across the pedestrian crossing on the main road and onto Percy Street. At the end of Percy Street go **R** to follow Clifford Street for just under 1km, past Ibrox parish church. Continue, following a ¶ **L** over the footbridge crossing the M8 to a T-junction with Urrdale Road and go **R**.

Coming to the main road at the end follow a ¶ **R** then **L** over the main road into Bellahouston Park. In the park there are many ¶ for the cycle route. If you find them a little confusing at junctions simply stick to the side of the path which the ¶ is on. These will lead you past the Art Lover's House and the Palace of Art to exit on the southern side of the

23

park onto Mosspark Boulevard. It's now time to leave the cycleway by going **L** onto this road and following it to the end and the T-junction with Dumbreck Road. Go **R** here and carefully across the next major roundabout, the site of the controversial M77 extension.

Just over the roundabout take the first minor road **R** past a ¶ for Dumbreck Riding School to follow part of the Burrell Walkway. Simply follow the main tarmac road after a **L** at the first T-junction, now sandwiched between Pollok grounds and Haggs Castle Golf Course to a T-junction facing the side of Pollok House. To the right are a number of attractions such as a sawmill and the White Cart Water. A **L** leads to a crossroads; here a left disappears into woods and right leads to the main entrance to Pollok House, a very worthwhile diversion.

After exploring the attractions of this area go straight through at this crossroads to bend left past a no entry to the front of the modern building housing the Burrell Collection. Again after exploring the diversions of this building follow on the tarmac road and **L** at the first split, staying on the tarmac road to exit at the traffic lights on Haggs Road. Go **L** here to the next major junction. Take the second **R** opposite another entrance to Pollok Park up Andrew's Drive. Shortly a small black gate on the **L** leads to Haggs Castle, housing an interesting museum.

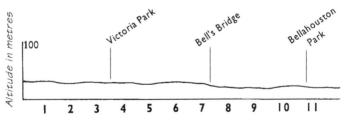

Turn round after a visit to the castle and straight over the main road and through the gateway into the park. Follow on the main track and past the lodge, remaining on the main track through the woods and past the fish pond. Following this main track you will recognise the junction you emerge at by Pollok House. From here you can pick up the track you entered the park on and retrace your outward route back to the Art Gallery.

Pollok House

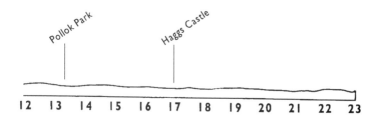

ALONG THE WAY

• **Glasgow Art Gallery and Museum** with free admission and a good cafe marks a suitable starting point to the journey and you can easily while away a few hours taking in its attractions at the start or finish. Impressive for both the red sandstone French Renaissance style exterior and the great open central atrium and adjoining courts and galleries inside, it houses natural and ethnic history collections and works of numerous famous painters amongst other attractions. The darkened stonework of the almost religious looking University of Glasgow can be seen on the opposite northern banks of the Kelvin. It's not difficult to see why this museum alone attracts nearly one million visitors a year.

• **Museum of Transport** Again with free admission, this museum has collections of all types of vehicle but perhaps the most poignant is the large collection of model ships. Many of the real things were made in the city and sunk in one of the world wars. The cafe inside is a good vantage point over much of the collection.

• **Clydeside and shipbuilding** An area once synonymous with a vast and powerful industry prior to world war one that all but collapsed after the second. However the area today is not merely a museum to former glory days. Henry Bell's pioneering steam driven Comet emerged from docks that more recently spawned 'Osprey One', the first sea-borne station that harnesses the energy of the waves. Controversially it was the brainchild of a private company, the government refusing to fund any research or development into this potentially revolutionary 'green' form of energy. Urban regeneration based on the service and leisure industry is now replacing the remnants of shipbuilding. Just crossing over Bell's Bridge the now empty area may be developed as part of a Millennium funded project including a multiplex cinema; such developments are set to change the face of Clydeside over the coming years.

• **The Clyde Port Authority Building and Meadowside Granary** The authority controls the Clyde below Glasgow including Greenock. They have the mammoth task of organising the huge quantities of trade on the Clyde - two-thirds of Scotland's foreign sea-borne trade passes through Clydeport. Meadowside Granary claims to be the biggest brick structure in the country.

• **Fossil Grove** in Victoria Park is centred around fossil trees and rocks some 330 million years old. Open Easter-September.

Finniston Crane

• **Pollok House** Everything you would expect of a powerful aristocrat's home and more; magnificent decor, one of the best collections of Spanish painting in the country and beautiful formal gardens combine with a former kitchen restored as a cafe. Admission free. Re-opening in summer 1996 after undergoing restoration.

• **The Burrell Collection** A huge range of all kinds of historical objects from throughout the centuries and across the globe were collected by one man, Sir William Burrell, and gifted to the city to form this superb collection. The only criteria for choosing objects seems to have been that he took a fancy to them! Objects from ancient and medieval societies are set alongside paintings from the 15th to the 19th centuries. Many of the interior features of historic buildings have actually been built into the fabric of a beautifully complementary modern building, in itself an attraction. (Daily 1000-1700, Sunday 1100-1700). Admission free.

• **Haggs Castle** Admission free, weekdays 1000-1700, Sunday 1100-1700. With children's displays and rooms restored to provide an interesting historical display of Mary Queen of Scots. Built in 1585 by John Maxwell, leading local aristocrat, it was superseded in the 18th century by Pollok House (see above).

2

PALACERIGG COUNTRY PARK

START Palacerigg Country Park   **Grid ref.** 788732

DISTANCE 19km/12miles

TIME ALLOWED 2-2½ hours with cafe break at the country park

GRADIENT DIFFICULTY Park section: 1;
Minor road section: some short but difficult grade 2/3 climbs.

TRACK SURFACE Most of the tracks within the country park are good wide cinder tracks - hard and level. Occasionally bumpy, rocky or muddy but the run shouldn't present any obstacle even to racers with a smaller number of gears.

ORDNANCE SURVEY MAP
Landranger 64, Glasgow; 65, Falkirk & West Lothian.
There is a useful orienteering map at the country park for 60p and numerous display boards.

ACCESS Off the B8054 south-east of Cumbernauld. **Car** Country Park car park. **Train** Cumbernauld station, 3km from the main entrance.

SUMMARY
The park section is ideal for younger children who can explore the tracks winding between woodland, moorland and animal enclosures in a traffic free environment (though watch out for occasional pony riders). The minor road section takes you through a hamlet, Glenhove, in the small wooded valley that houses the start of the Luggie Water. This section adds variety and distance and leads ultimately around the back of Fannyside Loch and into the country park. The small climbs on the road section shouldn't overface any cyclist beyond a beginner; they are short enough to push if you can't manage to pedal!

S Start in the car park at Palacerigg Country Park. In the top left hand corner of the car park as you enter it look for the sign through the trees indicating the way to the golf course and *no unauthorised vehicles*.

Immediately as you enter the trees bear **R** marked for the golf course and Fannyside. Ignore the next left (a cinder track over the golf course) and go straight on past the clubhouse. Just after this the road splits three ways; go straight on, ignoring the right behind the clubhouse and the left through woods. Stay on the main red cinder path for a while until a T-junction meeting Fannyside Loch, ahead and left of you.

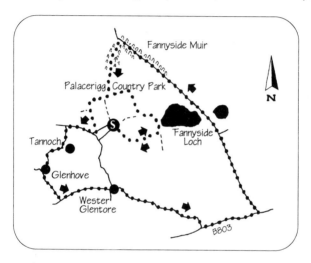

Go **L** at this T-junction and **R** at the next split to head northwards to another T-junction and **L** (Knowle Top deer park ¶ on the right). Take the next 90 degree turn to the **R** opposite a teeing off area on the golf course. Coming under pylons take an unmarked **L** onto a smaller track and follow the main obvious track past a couple of small lakes to a T-junction and **L** to pass back under pylons.

At the next main junction after crossing under pylons descend into Glencryan woods over a bridge, and ignoring tracks on both sides, bending to the left around a lake on your left. Follow the main track to the next junction and go **R.** Fork **L** bringing you to a junction with a tarmac road (ahead and to your left should be the European Bison enclosure). Go **R** here to a T-junction with the main road.

Go **R** onto the main road. Very shortly ignore a very minor left and take the next **L**. Drop quickly down past Tannoch stables and over the stream to climb into Glenhove. Take the first **L** in this small hamlet to another small brick bridge and climb for about ½km to a T-junction. Go **L** here and straight through a staggered crossroads at the next small settlement of Wester Glentore, continuing on this road to a T-junction with the main road. Go **L** onto the B803 leading towards Slamannan. Take the next tarmac road to the **L** in about 1km.

Follow this long, straight road for about 4km. After passing under electricity pylons look for an acute **L** back into the park, through a car barrier marked as a footpath. Follow under the pylons again after ignoring two right turns off the main track and past the sign back into the country park. Follow to a recognisable T-junction opposite a golf teeing off area and retrace your steps **L**, following your outward route by Fannyside Loch.

ALONG THE WAY
• **Palacerigg Country Park** *is really ideal for families or those with a like of unusual and exotic animals! The ride takes you through the great variety of landscape within the park including moorland, woodland and open grassland, a good change if you are tired of acres of cropped fields. Look out for unusual breeds such as European Bison, Prezwalski's Horses and Chamois. There is also plenty of wildlife roaming free, including deer. The park is open all day, every day and the visitor centre and cafe 1000-1800 (Summer - closed Tuesdays) and 1000-1630 (Winter - closed Mondays and Tuesdays).*

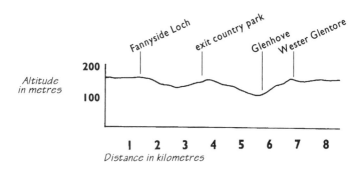

Bison, Palacerigg Country Park

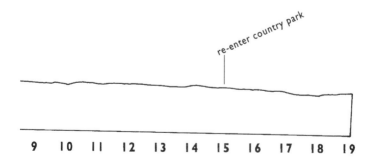

re-enter country park

9   10   11   12   13   14   15   16   17   18   19

3

AIRDRIE to BLACK HILL

START *Drumgelloch*   **Grid ref.** *778654*

DISTANCE *19km/12 miles*   **TIME ALLOWED** *2 -2½ hours*

GRADIENT DIFFICULTY *2 - fairly gradual gradients up to Black Hill*

TRACK SURFACE *A mix of easy wide Sustrans path, good wide farm track, and minor roads. A field and lift over a gate links two farm tracks. Small urban road section to return to Airdrie.*

ORDNANCE SURVEY MAP
*Landranger 64, Glasgow; 65, Falkirk & West Lothian
Sustrans leaflet - Airdrie to Bathgate railway path*

ACCESS *Start from Drumgelloch railway station, a line terminus in the east of Airdrie. Heading east from Airdrie centre on the A89 cross the roundabout with the A73. Shortly after this look for the small sign to the station on the right.* **Car** *park by the station.*

SUMMARY
Although beginning in the suburbs of Airdrie the Airdrie-Bathgate Sustrans path quickly leads to a very easy-on-the-eye rolling green landscape as you come to skirt the edge of Hillsend Reservoir. The climb towards Black Hill after Nether Bracco farm affords a good overview of your outward route by the reservoir, as you pass through hilly grassed farmland towards Lilly Loch. Although 270m (886ft) is the highest point reached, near Black Hill, the drop to Roughrigg Reservoir and the climb to Langside reveal that you are above many of the rolling hills interspersed with the Glasgow conurbation and its satellite towns laid out in front of you.

The only possible difficulty for beginners is the small field section and carry over a fence approaching Wester Bracco. Other than this some gradients can be long but none are really steep.

S The start of the Sustrans path is inside the station itself at the eastern terminus of the line, recognisable by the red information sign and bollards. Follow the Sustrans track under various bridges away from Airdrie into open countryside and to Plains, where the track crosses a minor road. At the other side of the road ignore the minor track going down to the right over a bridge. Stay on the main track out of Plains, crossing the A89.

Approaching Caldercruix the church tower comes into view and the track meets the bridge over the old line of the railway on the left. Going **R** you meet Caldercruix, Longrigend and Meadowfield church. Go **L** in front of it. Follow the road and before it swings left over a bridge look for the red Sustrans sign on the **R**.

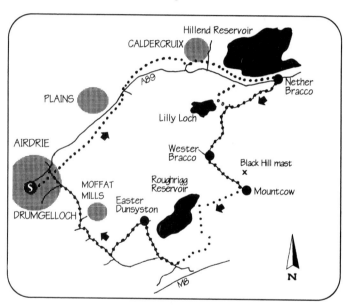

Staying on the track Hillend Reservoir appears on your left after a bridge. Follow the reservoir-side track for just over a kilometre until arriving at the whimsical sculpture on your left, entitled *Calorman Fishing*. Just before this you will have passed two green access bollards. Go through these and cross over the main road to the farm entrance to Nether Bracco opposite (possibly a dismount and scramble).

Take the concrete road through the gate and yet another in front of the farmhouse (*note this is signed as a private road. Sustrans indicate it on their leaflet as a possible linking route. If you encounter any problems you can use the right of way to the west. Go R on the A89 as you emerge opposite Nether Bracco, then L off the road up a right of way ¶ Lilly Loch. Follow south for about 1km and uphill. Join the farm track here and pick up directions below marked **).

Stay on the obvious main track through any closed gates and Lilly Loch comes into view after a short time, shielded by hills on the right. At the rights of way ¶ bear straight on the main track for Wester Bracco (* or R if you approached from the right of way to the north of Lilly Loch). The track ends at the junction of two grass fields. Go into the right hand one and follow its left hand side (heading more or less in a straight line away from Lilly Loch and towards a small brick hut, and further in the distance the mast at Black Hill). Lift the bike over the fence in the corner and immediately bear R in front of the hut and back onto the main track, following it to a T-junction at the public road opposite Wester Bracco farm.

Facing Wester Bracco go L onto the road and climb past the entrance to the Black Hill mast on the left. Shortly after this and over the brow of the hill, Mountcow farm comes into view. Just before it a farm track leads towards Roughrigg Reservoir in the distance. A right of way ¶

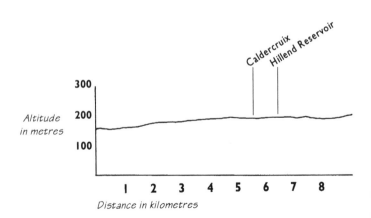

should point you **R** down this track to Salsburgh (although it was bent in the wrong direction on my last visit!). Lift your bike over the small gate and continue on 'across the tops'.

Shortly before descending close to the reservoir you cross the line of an old railway, banked steeply in places. Signs direct you back to Black Hill, right to Roughrigg Road and left to Salsburgh. Ignore these and carry straight on to cross over a concrete bridge across a reservoir feeder. Bend left and away from the reservoir, climbing slowly and bending right shortly after the M8 comes into view in front of you. Continue on past the farmhouse on your right to a staggered crossroads.

Go **R** at these staggered crossroads onto a quiet country road and **R** at the first split to Easter Dunsyston (basically a row of terraces). Through here the road bends left and a gravel track goes off the main road to the right, then through a farm. Follow the tarmac road downhill bearing right over Clattering Burn to a T-junction with a larger road, then go **R**. Go **L** at the next mini roundabout. Head through a modern housing development, past a school and hospital on the right to traffic lights at a bridge over the Sustrans route. Just over the bridge loop **L** 180 degrees to descend to the route under the bridge. Go **R** and retrace the Sustrans route back to Drumgelloch station.

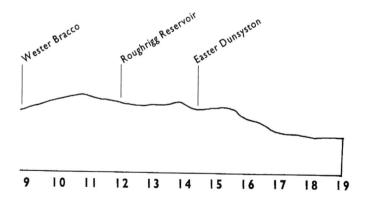

35

On the Airdrie-Bathgate Cycleway

4

VALE OF LEVEN

START Dumbarton   **Grid ref.** 398753

DISTANCE 22 km/13¾ miles   **TIME ALLOWED** 4 hours

GRADIENT DIFFICULTY
Grade 1 Sustrans path followed by a grade 3 road climb of 2km

TRACK SURFACE
Mainly Sustrans route with some minor road or track

ORDNANCE SURVEY MAPS
Landranger 63, Firth of Clyde

ACCESS Start from the Denny Tank Museum in Dumbarton. **Car** plenty of road parking in Dumbarton, and parking at the museum if you visit. **Train** The museum is 2 minutes from Dumbarton station.

SUMMARY
The Vale of Leven accommodates the river of the same name flowing south from Loch Lomond to join the Clyde. The broad, meandering river is left at Renton and in contrast a steep climb brings you over Carman Muir with great views of the Firth of Clyde. You can continue over the top and downhill for a look at the architectural oddity of Kilmahew House or you may curtail your journey at a suitable vantage point on Carman Muir, thus avoiding a steep climb back to this point.

S   Head away from the museum to the T-junction at the end of Castle Street and go **R**. Take the first **L** onto St. Mary's Way and follow the twisting street to Risk Street. Joining this street go **L** to the main road. Go **R** then immediate **L** down Bridge Street and over the bridge. Follow the road bending round right and before hitting the main road look for the cycle track ¶ **R** down to the riverside. By the information plaque at the river bear **L** under two bridges.

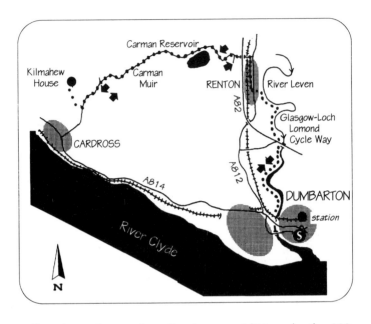

Follow the track away from Dumbarton outskirts under the A82. Shortly before a white footbridge ahead split off **L** on an unsigned path to the main street and go **R** (emerging just after the railway station on the left). Follow the main road through Renton for about ½ km and look for a **L** up Cardross Road. Climb steeply with excellent views left over the Vale of Leven. The road levels out by the raised grass banks

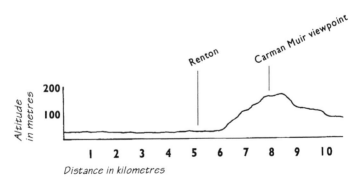

of Carman Reservoir on the left and views over the firth again open out as you start to drop after crossing the moor. Dropping through woods the second track on the **R** by the vandalised lodge provides *pedestrian* access to Kilmahew House through formal gardens.

Turn back on reaching the currently derelict building and follow your outward route back.

ALONG THE WAY

• **The Denny Tank Museum** *reflects the strong shipbuilding tradition of Dumbarton; the company whose name the museum bears were builders of the legendary Cutty Sark tea clipper now docked in Greenwich. It is in fact the last surviving part of Denny's shipyard. The main attraction of the museum is a fully restored and working ship model experiment tank. Open 1000-1600 (Sunday 1200-1600).*

• **The Vale of Leven** *has numerous historical connections. Tobias Smollet, the famous novelist is commemorated by a statue in Renton Schoolyard. The cycleway doubles as the Leven Valley Heritage Trail from Bowling to Balloch. There are numerous plinths with local background on; for example the last plinth before Renton gives interesting details of the last years Robert the Bruce spent in this area.*

•**Kilmahew House** *was once, believe it or not, a religious retreat, built by one of the most controversial architects of the day. There has been discussion as to whether this unique structure should have special protection and be rescued from its current collapsing state. There are also plans to develop the area into part housing, part country park, so something may be happening by the time you cycle this part.*

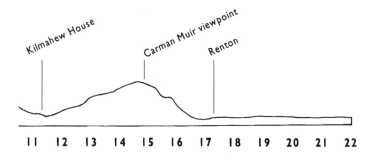

5

CUMBERHEAD FOREST

START Cumberhead Farm, near Coalburn (see access note below)
Grid Ref. 783347

DISTANCE 17km/10½ miles   **TIME ALLOWED** 3½ hours

GRADIENT DIFFICULTY 2/3

TRACK SURFACE Good wide forest tracks made to take heavy vehicles. Mountain bike recommended.

ORDNANCE SURVEY MAPS
Landranger 71, Lanark & Upper Nithsdale

ACCESS Up a farm track through the ruined South Cumberhead farm buildings. **Car** Parking is probably best in Coalburn. From here it is 5km to the start of the route. There is space for a handful of cars on the road up to South Cumberhead; any more may make passage for farm vehicles difficult. **Train** No nearby access: Lanark is the nearest, over 15km away.

SUMMARY
Being a little off the beaten track this route really gives you the feel of being away from it all. The 2,500 hectares of the Cumberhead Forest span the beautiful rolling hills at the northern edge of the Southern Uplands. Despite its isolated and wild feel it is easily accessed by car from the M74/A74 road south from Glasgow. The track winds through coniferous plantation, with intermittently good views to the north before ascending to Nutberry Hill. This is a fantastic viewpoint over the distinctive looking, hunched, grassy uplands to the west and even further north (to the Campsie Fells and other hills to the north of Glasgow) on a clear day.

Once in the middle of the forest there is no settlement for some miles, so be well prepared with food and drink and cold weather clothing if necessary. As always (and especially so in forested areas with few visible landmarks) a compass and knowledge of how to use it may be useful if you take the wrong turn.

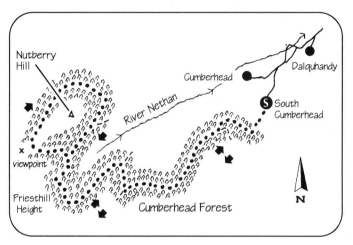

S Find the minor road running south west away from Lesmahagow and parallel to the river Nethan and follow it nearly to its end. After the turning ¶ left for Dalquhandy ignore two tracks on the right which lead to North Bankend Farm. At the next split bear **L**, taking you through the ruined farm buildings of South Cumberhead. Carrying on through a couple of gates and a field reach the edge of the forest. Go over the stile and onto the forest track.

At the first junction after 2km from the start of the run bear **R** keeping on the main track (the track to the left links to an access road from Douglas West: to access from Douglas West itself see Ordnance Survey map). After another 2km bear **R** at the next junction. Shortly after this go **L** staying on the main track, ignoring a minor split to the right.

The track now heads south west then turns round the top of a valley with good views from either side. After going over small feeder streams at the bottom of a descent climb to a junction and go **L**. The track climbs further and zigzags until, levelling out, it emerges out of the forest stage with fantastic views to the left. The actual summit of Nutberry Hill is about a kilometre to your right, north east off the track.

After the natural break point of Nutberry Hill carry on the track, which effectively circles the hill. There are further views as you start to head north east again. Coming nearly full circle and descending south west, ignore an acute track on the left and further descend to the junction from where you began the circuit of Nutberry Hill. Go **L** at this junction and follow the route you took outwards to this point.

ALONG THE WAY
• *Excellent views* are the main feature of this wild route. Although the scenery may lack the rugged grandeur of the Highlands further north, it more than makes up for this in the unusual, almost geometrically rounded form of many of the hills in this Southern Upland area. This is most apparent from **Nutberry Hill** looking down Leaze Burn, with Priesthill Height on the left and Spirebrush Hill on the right.

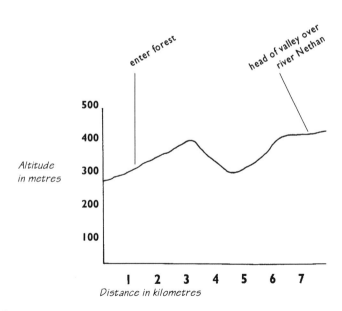

IMPORTANT NOTE

Shotton Forest Management, who manage Cumberhead Forest, have kindly negotiated permissive access to the forest tracks from the forest owners. Please note their following comments so that future access may continue. As always in the country relations between those owning and working the land and those seeking access is best preserved by considerately working together and respecting the owner's wishes;

A Bear in mind the forest is an active working forest, with activities such as timber operations and deer stalking taking place. Please take care and respect these activities.

B Under no circumstances should there be any camping during the fire danger period from early spring to mid-summer.

C The access points in this guide are those specified by the owners. No other access points should be used, despite that the fact that other tracks may appear to give access to the forest according to your map.

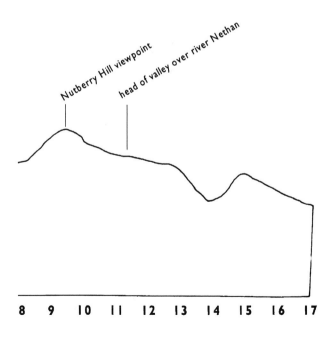

6

QUARRIER'S HOMES

START *Bridge of Weir*   **Grid ref.** *386656*

DISTANCE *18km/11 miles*   **TIME ALLOWED** *3 hours*

GRADIENT DIFFICULTY
Some hard grade 2 road climbs and about 6km of flat Sustrans path

TRACK SURFACE *Minor roads and Paisley-Greenock cycle route*

ACCESS *You can join the Sustrans route from many places in Bridge of Weir town centre.* **Car** *town centre parking.* **Train** *Johnstone station (using part of the Paisley to Irvine spur to link north if you wish) is about 6km from Bridge of Weir.*

ORDNANCE SURVEY MAP
*Landranger 63, Firth of Clyde
(also 64, Glasgow, for access from Johnstone)*

SUMMARY
Although the smooth surfaces on this route mean an off-road bike is not essential, the lower gears are still useful for a few of the longer steepish climbs above Bridge of Weir. The minor roads above Bridge of Weir give you a good chance to take in the countryside, followed by the interesting story of the picturesque Quarrier's Homes.

S There are a number of places to pick up the Sustrans route in Bridge of Weir town centre. Follow it south east to cross under the A761 Johnstone Road and into countryside away from the town centre. Just after crossing over the first minor road head off the access point to your **L**, and **L** again at the junction with the minor road to arrive at a crossroads with the A761 by Bridge Motors.

Carry straight on over the main road onto Locher Road. At the first T-junction at the top of the climb go **L,** then shortly after coming into Kilbarchan first **R.** After passing under pylons take the second fork **R** (the first goes to a farm). Go **R** at the next crossroads and first **L** after dropping down and going over the bridge at Locher Water. At the next split go **R** (campsite signed straight on possibly). Pass beautiful houses with splendid dovecotes at Barnbeth and continue on the road through a golf course, with good views over to the left later on. Descend to the back of Bridge of Weir on Clevans Road to a T-junction and go **L.**

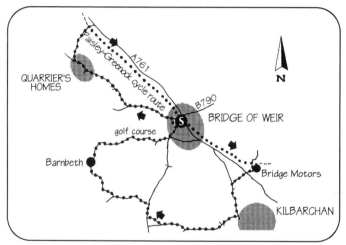

Now in a rich residential area of Bridge of Weir, take the second **L** at a staggered crossroads down Horsewood Road. At a T-junction go **L** away from Bridge of Weir. Split off **R** at the first opportunity ¶ *Quarrier's Homes.* The main cluster of orphans' houses are on the right signed alongside the coffee house. Continue out of the village on the main road and go **R** as you exit the village.

Follow the road for about 4km, over a bridge at the River Gryfe to a second bridge before the main road. Split off **L** before the bridge through gates to the Paisley-Greenock Sustrans route, and go **R** onto the route itself. Pass the innovative sculpture *XVII Legion* and continue back into Bridge of Weir, entering on a high old viaduct, with good views over weirs to the right.

ALONG THE WAY

•**Quarriers Village** contains a miniature 'village' within the wider community - part of a charitable organisation originally founded by William Quarrier in 1878. Born in Glasgow to a poor family the young Quarrier was deeply impressed by the poverty he saw in his first job in a hat pin factory at just six years old, and later as an apprentice boot and shoe maker.

His own successful business allowed him to express his charitable intentions. First he founded 'Industrial Brigades'; destitute young people were given a uniform and shoe shining equipment and allowed to keep the profits of their labours. The village homes at Quarrier's allowed house fathers and mothers to provide homes to orphans from all over Scotland. Today the charity has diversified and modernised into a number of areas including running an epilepsy centre and a stop-over for homeless people in Glasgow.

Quarrier's encourages people to visit the village. There is a gift and coffee shop and temporary museum in the Mount Zion Church (to move at some time in the future to a larger heritage centre). The village itself with its original 'Cottage Homes' devised by Quarrier still retains the neat, compact ambience that so many orphans have been raised in.

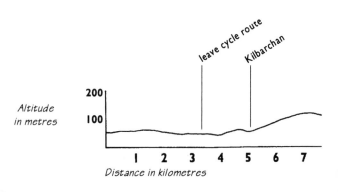

Carron Valley Reservoir (Route 7, overleaf)

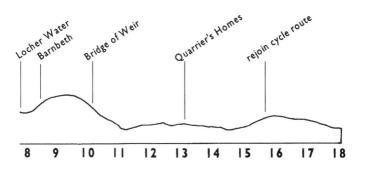

7

CARRON VALLEY

START Carron Valley Forest   **Grid ref.** 718837

DISTANCE 14km/8¾ miles   **TIME ALLOWED** 1½ -2 hours

GRADIENT DIFFICULTY An easy rolling grade 2

TRACK SURFACE Good wide Forestry Commission tracks. A little rocky in places.

ORDNANCE SURVEY MAP Landranger 57, Stirling & the Trossachs

ACCESS Start from the Forestry Commission car park off the B818 west of Carron Bridge. Head west on the B818 away from the M80 and along the Carron Valley. At a minor crossroads go straight on past the Carron Bridge Hotel. Shortly after this bend left and over a bridge. The car park is shortly on the left and is unsignposted from the road, over a small bridge. **Train** Stirling station is17km/10½ miles away.

SUMMARY
The Carron Valley lies sandwiched between the Kilsyth Hills to the south and small groups of hills to the north (including the Fintry Hills and Cairnoch Hill) and you can experience the grand scenery on this relatively easy run without any really strenuous climbs. The outward leg of this Forestry Commission run rises slightly to round the foot of 'Little Bin' hill before dropping towards the Western end of the dam. There are fine views back down the dam and of Craigannet, Cairnoch and Fintry Hills to the north. Bear in mind the safety comments in the main introduction regarding riding in forestry areas.

S Take the main track from the car park ignoring any left turns in the car park area. As the dam wall comes into sight go straight on over a minor crossroads (right goes down to a gate in front of the dam). Bend round right ignoring two left turns and the dam comes into sight on the right, with good views over it to the white-washed houses at its head.

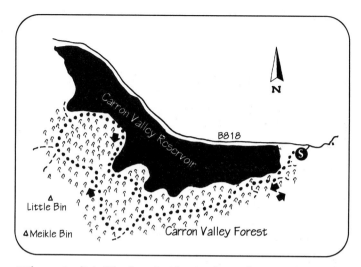

At the next split in ½km bear **R**. After another 2½km just over a bridge bear **L**. This will take you around the base of 'Little Bin', the wooded hillside in front. The larger, unwooded hilltop is 'Meikle Bin' ('Meikle' meaning big). Shortly fork **R** again. After following the base of Little Bin for another 2½km go **R** then **R** again at the next two junctions in succession.

Follow the track downhill, and **R** at the next fork to bring you onto a track with beautiful views over Carron Valley Reservoir on the left. Follow the track alongside the reservoir and then into the woods. Meet the next junction just over a bridge and bear **L** over another bridge. Continue back for nearly 4km, now retracing your outward steps, bearing **L** at every opportunity to the car park.

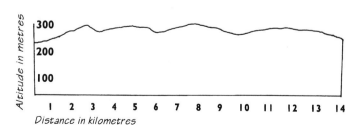

8

MUGDOCK COUNTRY PARK

START *Clachan of Campsie*

Grid ref. *611795*

DISTANCE *21km/13 miles*

TIME ALLOWED *3½ hours*

GRADIENT DIFFICULTY *Grade 1 railway path and country park with some grade 2 road climbs in between.*

TRACK SURFACE *Excellent quality cinder path on the Strathkelvin Railway Path and good quality tracks in Mugdock Country Park combine with minor roads.*

ORDNANCE SURVEY MAP *Landranger 64, Glasgow*
Also location map in the country park.

ACCESS *Start in front of the art gallery in Clachan of Campsie, north of the A891 just out of Lennoxtown, heading towards Strathblane.* **Car** *Small parking area in front of the art gallery.* **Train** *No easy rail link. Milngavie station is 11km away using A81 and A891.*

SUMMARY

Easy to medium difficulty with a few testing climbs and one small section on 'A' road through Strathblane (it is possible to cut this out by weaving through houses behind A81 in Strathblane). Certainly this route has much to offer; spectacular views of the Campsie Fells and the small valley lying between them and Lennoxtown Forest combine with a beautiful panorama before entering Mugdock Country Park.

The park itself is packed with history, with two castles amidst an abundantly wooded natural habitat housing a variety of wildlife. The visitor centre in the country park carries a wide selection of leaflets and the Ranger Service can advise on other suitable routes for cyclists.

50

S From the parking ground in Clachan of Campsie take the road back to the T-junction with the A891 and go **L**. Shortly, opposite a white group of old houses on the left, look for entry to the railway path on the **R** over a small bridge. Go **L** on the path and continue to a junction following ¶ *Strathblane* **R**. A very pleasant path leads through woods and under a bridge past the rocky knoll of Dunglass on the left. Follow the path to its end, bending right as you enter Strathblane to exit on the main road opposite a church. Go **L** to a T-junction with the A81.

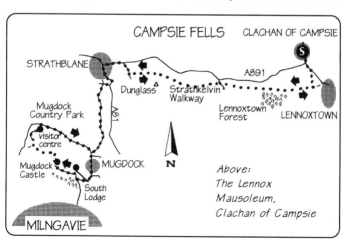

Above:
The Lennox
Mausoleum,
Clachan of Campsie

Go **L** again and climb, winding away from the village. After climbing a steep right hand hairpin take the next **R** down Milngavie Road ¶ *Children's Hospital*. Go **L** at the crossroads and follow the road straight on for nearly 2km (superb views behind you) then **L** ¶ *Mugdock village* (not immediate left for Glasgow on A81), passing through the village itself. Stay on this road through the village and exiting it bend right to a superb view over Mugdock Reservoir and Milngavie. Shortly after this take a **R** ¶ *Mugdock Country Park*, to the South Lodge Entrance.

Pass through the gates to the country park, go **L** at a T-junction and split **R** as Mugdock Castle comes into view. After a look at the castle carry on down the left hand side of the castle, keeping the building on your right and fork **L** ¶ *Visitor Centre & Craigend Castle*. In the woods fork **L** to a T-junction with the main track and **L** again. Pass over the crossroads in the woods to Craigend Castle, going to the right of this building (ignore left for Khyber car park). Pick up the track to the left of the visitor centre and car park to exit at the road. Go **R** onto this road and in just over 1km pick up the **L** which you will recognise as the road you entered Mugdock village from. Use your outward route back to Clachan of Campsie, with equally splendid views on the return.

ALONG THE WAY
• *Clachan of Campsie is a delightful small village nestling at the foot of the locally popular Campsie Glen. It is easy to let the small row of shops in the centre, including art gallery and bike shop, distract you*

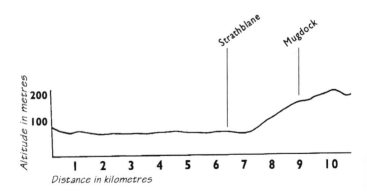

from the real star of the scene, the ruined church set in an ancient looking graveyard, absolutely full of atmosphere. Hearsay has it that St. Machan first brought Christianity to the area and constructed a rudimentary church. The current ruined church is reputed to be on the site of the saint's grave. Look out also for the mausoleum of the long standing local aristocrats, the Lennox family.

• **The Strathkelvin Railway Walkway,** also suitable for disabled users and cycles, follows the old route of a combination of railway lines. The Monkland & Kirkintilloch Railway took coal from the former area to the Forth & Clyde Canal at Kirkintilloch from where it could be transported to the Clyde or Lothian sea outlets. The part followed by this particular ride was once a branch line of the Edinburgh & Glasgow Railway that headed off north from Lenzie through Lennoxtown, with a later extension through the Blane valley to Killearn and Aberfoyle, and as in many such cases alas the line is no more! Closure to passengers in the 1950's was followed by closure to goods in the 60's.

• **Mugdock Country Park** is a fittingly diverse and interesting end to the ride with two castles (interiors not open), visitor centre, tea room, gift shop and craft units. (call 0141-9566100 for opening hours). If you decide to explore outside the suggested route, please note and stick to the permissive cycletracks given on the information boards.

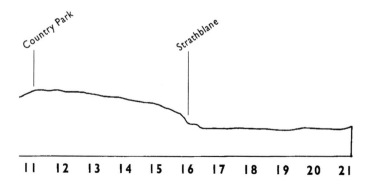

• **Mugdock Castle** reflects the history of one of Scotland's foremost aristocratic families, the Grahams. In the 14th century they allied with other families against the fiercely anti-English Robert the Bruce. Best surviving remnant of the first stone castle on this site is the south west tower, now under restoration. Perhaps the height of the family's power came in the mid 15th century when their Stirlingshire lands became the Barony of Mugdock, with the castle as their central power base. Look out for the keyhole shape openings in the wall designed to take guns as opposed to the old traditional weapon of bow and arrow.

The 17th century saw the start of a series of events that secured the family a major place in Scottish history; the fifth earl of Montrose, the Great Marquis, lead the Covenanters (Scottish protesters who resented the attempted introduction of a new prayer book) against Charles I, but switched sides to fight with the king against another powerful local noble, the Duke of Argyll. The end result was that the fifth earl was betrayed and executed in Edinburgh and the castle fell into Argyll's hands.

Although later recovered by the family, Mugdock Castle never really regained it former glory and became the home of a minor branch of the family. In the 19th century a Georgian mansion on the site was later superseded by a Scots-baronial mansion before the park was gifted to Central Regional Council for country park development.

Originally Graham land, **Craigend Estate,** on which **Craigend Castle** is now built, passed in the seventeenth century to the Smith family as a reward for military service the family had given to the 'Great Marquis' (although the Smith family still had to pay for this land they had lived on since 1500!).

The castle you pass before reaching the visitor centre is better preserved and more modern in appearance than Mugdock (early 19th century in fact). With the purchase of the land the Smith family climbed socially to become yeoman farmers (previously being in the service of the Grahams, possibly as armourers and blacksmiths). The estate had an interesting variety of owners after the Smiths including an ambassador, newspaper magnate, shipbuilder and a family who opened a zoo here after world war two. Although the zoo closed in 1956 it has retained its fame to today as 'Charlie the Elephant' attempted to follow its owner into a local pub after working hours and became lodged in the doorway.

9

FORTH & CLYDE CANAL

START *Kirkintilloch*   **Grid ref.** *655736*

DISTANCE *17km/10½ miles*

TIME ALLOWED *An easy 2 hours*   **GRADIENT DIFFICULTY** *1*

TRACK SURFACE
Cinder canal towpath; flat but may be a little muddy after heavy rain.

ORDNANCE SURVEY MAP *Landranger 64, Glasgow*

ACCESS *Kirkintilloch main street runs north-south parallel to the A8006 and the Luggie Water just to the east.* **Car** *Car park in the Caprice car park at the top of the main street.* **Train** *Lenzie station is about 2½km/1½ miles from the start.*

SUMMARY
Flat and easy; ideal for Dutch cyclists! This section of the Forth & Clyde Canal stretches through leafy green country, whilst the Campsie Fells rise alluringly to the north. Canal boats converted to restaurants ply the stretch of the canal after Glasgow Bridge and if you are lucky you may see one steering the narrow course through the bridge at Cadder. At Possil Loch countryside gives way to the urban fringes of Glasgow, so simply turn round and enjoy a whole new set of views coming the other way. An ideal family run and suitable for most types of bike. A British Waterways permit is needed to cycle on the towpath: consult canal riding advice in introduction.

S From the Caprice car park you can visit the Auld Kirk and Barony Chambers before heading down the High Street. Just after the parish church on the left take the **R** hand towpath by the canal, keeping the canal on your left. Very soon you are in open country, following the towpath straight down to the moorings and pub at Glasgow Bridge. Continuing on, the delightful cottages and church surrounding the

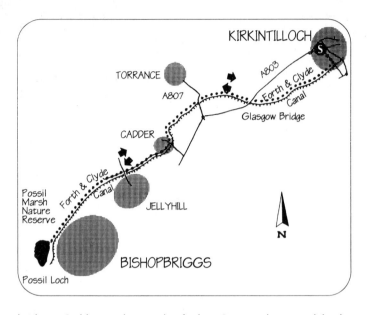

bridge at Cadder are about 2½km further. Carry on the towpath by the ivy covered cottage, over the road here, after a look around. The countryside opens out after this and after crossing a road the real end of the greenery is marked at Possil Loch opposite the power sub station at Bishopbriggs. You probably won't be able to see the loch as it has become full of plants and access is difficult.

Turn round and retrace your steps back at any point you fancy after Bishopbriggs comes into view.

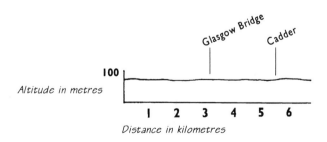

By the Forth & Clyde Canal, Cadder

ALONG THE WAY

• **The Auld Kirk and Barony Chambers** are right by the Caprice car park at the top of the main shopping street in Kirkintilloch. The Auld Kirk is now a museum with displays on local historic activities such as boatbuilding. Constructed in the early nineteenth century the Barony Chambers served as Town Hall, court house, jail and school.

• **The Forth & Clyde Canal** now only partially open to craft, ran 38 miles and linked the Clyde at Bowling in the west to Grangemouth, on the Forth, in the east. The highest point of the waterway lies at 156ft above sea level and requires 39 locks. There are pleasure cruises from May to September or boats for charter all year round (contact Canal Society for details: 0141-7763812)

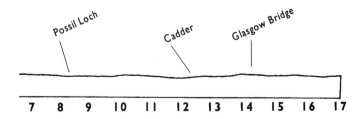

10

PORT GLASGOW & KILMACOLM

START Port Glasgow   **Grid ref.** 318744

DISTANCE 28km/17½ miles   **TIME ALLOWED** 4/5 hours

GRADIENT DIFFICULTY
A rolling 2. The route is quite long though and some climbs extended.

TRACK SURFACE Part of the Paisley to Greenock cycle route is combined with minor roads

ORDNANCE SURVEY MAP
Landranger 63, Firth of Clyde
There is also a useful town map of Port Glasgow, Gourock & Greenock and one of Bridge of Weir & Kilmacolm, both in the Nicolson Street Guide series.

ACCESS Start from Birkmyre Park, which sits atop the town above the station, straddling rolling country and the housing developments of this post-industrial port on the A8, south of the Firth of Clyde. **Car** Suitable road parking near Birkmyre Park. **Train** Port Glasgow station is literally a few streets away from the start of the route.

SUMMARY
The ridge of the hill above Port Glasgow makes an ideal point from which to survey the Firth of Clyde below, as it starts to yawn out between Gare Loch and Greenock, with especially good views of the docks and waterside features of Port Glasgow and Greenock. The hardest part is perhaps the initial climb to the Sustrans route and a last extended climb on the return leg to Kilmacolm. Whilst the climbs don't require a great level of fitness in themselves, combined with the overall length they mean that at least a reasonable level of fitness is advisable. One to take easy and savour the views on a fine clear day.

S In Birkmyre Park find the very top path (actually the Sustrans route), running east through the top of the park. Follow the path out of the park to cross a road (Barrs Brae) to the back of a housing estate. Shortly after this the route splits; go **R,** actually signed on the tarmac surface for Kilmacolm.

Follow the obvious cycle track until it meets a road at Crosshill Road. Cross straight over and follow over another main road, now climbing up Montrose Avenue. Pick up the cinder track of the cycle track on your **R** by a farmhouse on the right. The track bends round to a T-junction and go **R** here. Simply follow it through a cutting and under bridges then onto Kilmacolm, with its distinctive church spire in the distance, emerging there at Whitelea Crescent.

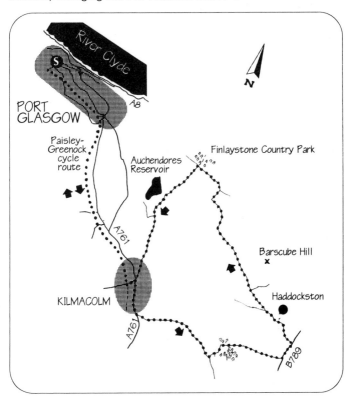

Follow Whitelea Crescent to the first **L** and up Whitelea Court housing development. Look for a narrow passage on the left, leading through to a small cul de sac, emerging into it by the Sustrans sign for the cycle route. Go **R** here to the main road and **R** through and out of the town centre area. Follow this Bridge of Weir Road, out through leafy suburbs. Go **L** down Porterfield Road and next **R** down Glencairn Road. Go **L** at the T-junction at the end.

Follow this road out through a golf course and go **L** at the first unsigned fork, staying on this narrow potholed road until meeting a 'B' road and go **L**. Take the next **L** ¶ *Haddockston House* and after meeting this house go **R** at the next split. Go **L** at a further split and downhill with the opposite bank of the firth coming into view after a while. Follow to a T-junction with a larger but still quiet road and go **L** onto it.

You may want to drop in at Finlaystone Country Park on the right shortly. Just after the country park a **L** will put you on a minor road ascending through the back of Kilmacolm to a junction with the main road, after about 3km, passing Auchendores Reservoir on the way. Cross straight over the main road here and down a minor road to the right of the library. You will recognise the narrow passageway on the **L** which takes you down Whitelea Court and **R** down Whitelea Crescent to pick up the cycle track back to the start.

ALONG THE WAY
• **Port Glasgow** *itself originated in the seventeenth century when there was no deep water berth near the city centre, so this place was originally exactly what its name suggests. When the Clyde was deepened further upstream it turned to shipbuilding. Near the centre of the town is a replica of the Comet, a steamship designed by Henry Bell of Helensburgh that serviced Glasgow and Greenock from 1812 until 1820 when she was wrecked.*

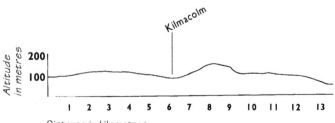

Distance in kilometres

Looking over Port Glasgow to Ardmore Point

Further up the coast you also get a good viewpoint of **Greenock**, once built around the herring trade, then shipbuilding! Nowadays its most notable features are the cranes and derricks that litter its skyline. If you visit the centre the McLean Museum has a number of James Watt relics, for the inventor of steam power was born here.

• **Finlaystone Country Park** Finlaystone House, within the country park, is where John Knox first dispensed the Sacrament according to the rites of the Reformed Church. He was one of a group of protestant Scottish puritans during Elizabeth I's reign who helped her oppose the Catholic threat of the French Queen Mother attempting to gain control of the Scottish government. It's also a nice place to have a coffee break and a wander in the grounds.

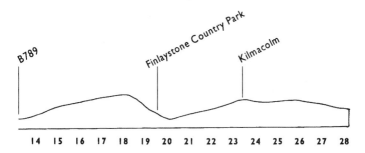

11
GARADHBAN FOREST

START *Drymen*   **Grid Ref.** *474885*

DISTANCE *17km/10½ miles*   **TIME ALLOWED** *3 hours*

GRADIENT DIFFICULTY *2/3*

TRACK SURFACE *Good quality forestry track and minor roads*

ORDNANCE SURVEY MAP
Landranger 57, Stirling & the Trossachs

ACCESS *Drymen is ideally situated between the Campsie Fells and Loch Lomond, west of the A809.* **Car** *Free parking outside the tourist information office on Balmaha Road.* **Train** *No nearby access.*

SUMMARY
Its proximity to stunning mountain scenery and the famed 'bonnie banks' mean Drymen is squarely on the tourist trail. As an added bonus for the town the immensely popular West Highland Way passes nearby. This route covers part of this trail which may be busy in summer months so please give way to pedestrians. It offers plenty of splendid scenery with views of the Campsie Fells and Loch Lomond itself, with climbs of mainly moderate difficulty.

S From the the tourist office head back to the T-junction with the Main Street. Go up this main road to the square then **L** at the top of the square by the Clachan Inn onto Old Gartmore Road. Soon out in the country the road becomes single track and climbs to the corner of the Forestry Commission's Garadhban Forest. Split **L** off the road here onto the forest track (about 2km after leaving Drymen).

A short distance on this track go **L** at the T-junction and shortly bear **R** back into the forest (just before the vehicle barrier on the track ahead). Split **L** and continue to a T-junction and go **L** to a gate. Through the gate follow the obvious grass track to another gate at the bottom corner of the woods and follow the track which keeps the woods on your right, all the while with stunning views over Loch Lomond. The broad sweep of the loch and westerly mountains confronts you just after going **R** at the next T-junction.

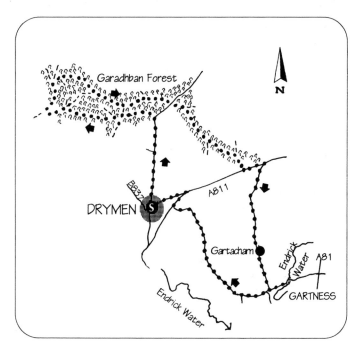

Climb back into the heart of the forest on this track to a crossroads and go **R** onto the West Highland Way. Follow the main track ignoring several turnings down to the right and emerging at a minor road by the car park, nearly 5km after joining the West Highland Way. Go **L** onto the road and immediate **R** again picking up the long distance 'Way' as the Campsie Fells jut out ahead of you. Split **R** then **L** through the forest to come to a T-junction with pylons rising up on the other side. **R** here brings you to the A811 and go **L** onto this main road. Again there are good views of the western end of the Campsies; look out especially for the locally well known 'Notch of Dumgoyne'.

On the main road follow the next minor road **R** ¶ *Gartacharn Farm*. About 2½km down this road come to a T-junction with a road. A ten minute ride to the left here brings you to pretty cottages at Gartness next to a picturesque weir on the Endrick Water. **R** will take you homewards to the A811 in about 3km, going **R** then first **L** onto the B858 back to Drymen and the square.

ALONG THE WAY

• **Drymen** Derived from the Gaelic meaning 'little ridge', Drymen is now a major centre for hikers as the West Highland Way passes very close by before reaching Loch Lomond at Balmaha. The straightness of the road you take up to Garadhban Forest suggests it was a military road built shortly after the Jacobite rising of 1745.

• **The Pots Of Gartness** are the rocky pools round which the tiny hamlet itself is situated. Known as a good spot to watch salmon leaping in spring and autumn.

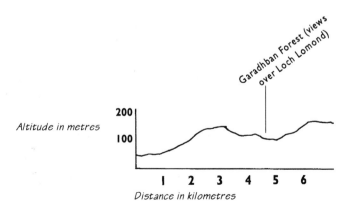

*Looking over Loch Lomond
from the Garadhban Forest*

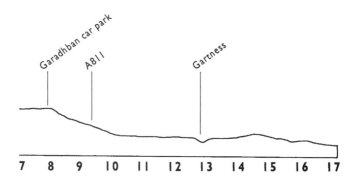

12

CROY & BAR HILLS

START *Auchinstarry*   **Grid ref.** *719771*

DISTANCE *10km/6¼ miles*   **TIME ALLOWED** *2 hours*

GRADIENT DIFFICULTY
2/3 climbing Croy and Bar Hills, with return by canal path grade 1

TRACK SURFACE
A lot of green track over the hill tops is quite tiring, especially the push up to the hill fort at Bar Hill. Canal towpath and a small road section.

ORDNANCE SURVEY MAP
Landranger 64, Glasgow; also display at picnic area

ACCESS *Start from Auchinstarry picnic area on the B802 between Cumbernauld and Kilsyth, just after crossing over the Forth & Clyde Canal and the River Kelvin.* **Car** *park at Auchinstarry picnic area.* **Train** *Croy station is less than a couple of kilometres from the start.*

SUMMARY
'Short and hard, but rewarded with great viewpoints' is possibly the best one line description of this ride! The hill climbs are quite tough propositions even for reasonably fit bikers, and being partly on grass are more tiring than you might expect. The climb to Bar Hill involves lifting your bike over 4-5ft high gates so make sure you are capable of this before attempting this run. There is a small and very steep grass section before Bar Hill fort where you might also have a tough push.

Having uttered these words of warning there are really superb views from the tops of both hills and it is worth taking it slowly but steadily up the hills and taking your time to rest and enjoy the views down the Kelvin Valley and across to the Kilsyth Hills and Campsie Fells. Definitely one for those who have plenty of gears! If you find the route a little short, link it to the Colzium House run for a longer outing.

S From Auchinstarry picnic area car park follow one of the tracks that lead east away from the road, with the lake slightly above you on your right. The wide gravel path narrows after passing the end of the lake. Follow the straight tree-lined path to a T-junction with the road and go **R**. Bear **R** at every opportunity to cross over a small river and then the canal bridge. Climb the hill and on the brow look for the white coloured ancient monument sign to the **R** for the Antonine Wall and Croy Hill. Follow this wide farm track through a gate and under pylons to a T-junction of rough tracks and go **L.**

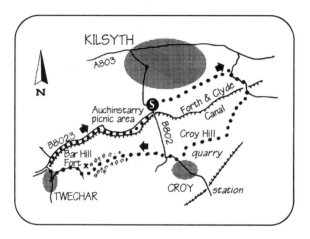

Follow this until you meet the monument sign. This gives details about the construction of the Antonine Wall at this point, and of the remains of Croy fort further on. Bear **R** up the obvious green track; the remains of the wall on the right of this track are obvious. Follow it up to the cluster of trees, passing to the left of these and to the right of a brick ruin, through two large stones. The green track then bears away from the quarry, which is over a drop on the left, and between two hillocks to a good viewpoint above trees on the opposite side of the hill.

From this viewpoint the track heads straight for the back of the housing estate at Croy; head for the right hand corner of this where you will find a black metal pedestrian entrance. Exit here and in the open area bear left, exiting onto Nethercroy Road to the T-junction with Constarry Road.

Go **R** onto Constarry Road and to a T-junction with the busy main road (B802). Go **R** downhill here and in 20-30 metres look for the **L** by a white ancient monument sign for Antonine Wall/Bar Hill in half a mile, down a wide hardpacked track. Through a black gate, lift over and continue through woods approaching an open area. Follow the wide mown grass area straight ahead to the narrower grass track between the conifers. This narrows then and eventually you push up a steep grass hill. Atop the hill the track goes right and hairpins left to round a wall in front of you. On the right is a large, open grassy area housing the remains of Bar Hill fort with informative signs.

PLEASE DON'T RIDE AROUND THIS AREA - IT IS A BEAUTIFULLY MAINTAINED HISTORIC MONUMENT. Dismount and wheel your bike around the left hand edge of the site. After a look round and rest you can press on with a carry over the black gate in the corner of the field to a T-junction of tracks by a circular water installation ahead on the left. Go **R** at this junction and downhill to the main road in Twechar by a church and memorial.

At this T-junction bear **R** and through Twechar to the T-junction over the canal bridge. The pavement on the **R** immediately over the bridge becomes the towpath by the canal - *but beware this is predominantly a single track, so give way to pedestrians and on the initial stages watch for the drop on the left towards the road.* This quiet section ends at the Auchinstarry bridge where you meet a road T-junction. **L** takes you back to the picnic site over the river bridge, on the **R.**

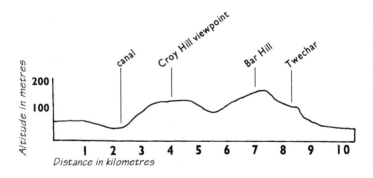

ALONG THE WAY

• **The Antonine Wall** is evident along much of Croy Hill and at the fort on Bar Hill. The Romans only made one substantial incursion into Scotland, during which time this turf rampart on a stone base was built to deter the Picts and Scots. The short straw of manning what must then have seemed the last defence against a barbaric, foe-ridden no man's land was drawn by (or rather given to) auxiliary troops of the Roman Empire such as Gauls, Rhinelanders, Thracians and Syrians (whose archers manned the fort at Bar Hill).

You can get an idea of the scale of much of the turf rampart along the top of Croy Hill; imagine having this meagre earth ramp as the only line of defence between you and hundreds of less than friendly warriors! The fort at Bar Hill may seem a little more comforting having housed bathhouses, barrack blocks and granaries. The wall was abandoned after only twenty years around 185 AD, as the Romans fell back upon Hadrian's Wall to the south.

The Campsie Fells from Croy Hill

13

BANTON LOCH & COLZIUM HOUSE

START *Auchinstarry*   **Grid ref.** *719771*

DISTANCE *12km/7½ miles*

TIME ALLOWED *2 hours with a visit to Colzium House*

GRADIENT DIFFICULTY *A very easy 2 with some grade 1 towpath*

TRACK SURFACE *Canal towpath, hardpacked tracks, minor roads*

ORDNANCE SURVEY MAP *Landranger 64, Glasgow;
useful maps on display board at the picnic area*

ACCESS *Start from Auchinstarry picnic area on the B802 between
Cumbernauld and Kilsyth, just after crossing the Forth & Clyde Canal
and the River Kelvin. **Car** park at Auchinstarry picnic area. **Train** Croy
station is less than a couple of kilometres from the start. In fact you
may pick up the canal before reaching the picnic area.*

SUMMARY
*The Forth & Clyde Canal near Auchinstarry is full of interesting water
borne plants and backed by dramatic sloping woods. Be aware that
you require a British Waterways permit to use these paths (see the
introduction on how to obtain a permit and general advice).*

*A relatively short ride, and one to take quite leisurely to enjoy the rich
valley and loch countryside and the unusual delights of Colzium
House. The tracks present no special difficulties but please give way
on the off-road rights of way sections to pedestrians, as they are a little
narrow. The path by Banton Loch may be busy so it may be best to
dismount if this is so. Ideal for family groups.*

S The Auchinstarry picnic area lies on the north of the River Kelvin just before entering Kilsyth proper. If you have parked in the picnic area come back out onto the main road and go **L**. Shortly after the bridge over the Kelvin take the **L** onto the towpath on the left hand side of the canal, keeping the canal on your right. Carry on this path, crossing over the road at the next bridge and staying on the same bank. The valley opens out now in contrast to the wooded hillside of Croy Hill which you passed earlier on the right. You will have been following the electricity pylons on your left for about 2km when they swing away left over a field. Shortly after they take this turn of direction notice an unsignposted small footpath on your **L**.

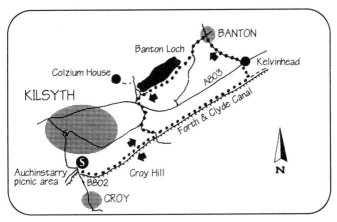

Climb this small grassy path passing through a couple of gates, and giving way to any pedestrians. Climb to meet the main A803 joining Glasgow and Linlithgow. Go **R** onto the main road then immediate **L** up a more minor road ¶ Banton. In the village centre take the **L** opposite the Swan Inn and in about ½km look for a small unsignposted track (starting as tarmac and turning to hardpacked cinder) between houses on the **R**. This follows Banton Loch's south shore.

Bear **R** at two junctions towards the end of the loch, bringing you round the western end of the loch and **L** just before a small bridge. This brings you to a track junction within the Colzium estate. **R** will take you up towards the main attractions, and after visiting the house for possible refreshment you may pick up the track to your **L** at this junction back to the main A803.

Bowling Basin (Route 14 - across)

Go **L** onto the main road and first **R** ¶ *Dullatur 1½*. Ignore the right for Kilsyth and stay on your chosen road to bring you to a bridge over the canal you crossed on your outward leg. Go **R** back onto the towpath just before the bridge. You can now retrace your steps to the next canal bridge and **R** to the picnic area.

ALONG THE WAY
• **Colzium House** is a pleasant detour after you emerge from Loch Banton. As well as a former mansion house, now museum, the estate contains unusual features such as walled ornamental garden, curling pond (reputedly the oldest in the UK) and theatre. Also see the ruins of the earlier Colzium Castle. A good opportunity to take a break in their cafe.

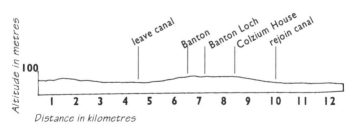

⟨ 14 ⟩

DUMBARTON CASTLE

START *Clydebank*   ***Grid ref.*** *478715*

DISTANCE *22km/13¾ miles*   ***TIME ALLOWED*** *4 hours*

GRADIENT DIFFICULTY *1*

TRACK SURFACE *Mainly the Glasgow-Loch Lomond cycle route, which is good cinder track. A few small road sections which can be 'pushed' if necessary.*

ORDNANCE SURVEY MAPS
Landranger 64, Glasgow

ACCESS *Pick up the cycleway as it runs along the south bank of the Forth & Clyde Canal near the Mountblow area of Clydebank. The A814 west from Glasgow to Dumbarton runs close to the cycle route at this point.* **Car** *on-road parking off the A814 in this area.* **Train** *Dalmuir station is a few minutes' ride.*

SUMMARY
Although this route runs in the shadow of the Kilpatrick Hills for much of its length, man-made rather than natural features are really the highlight. Ancient and modern are represented respectively by the finishing point of Dumbarton Castle and the huge engineering feat of the Erskine Bridge (an excursion over the top of this can be made an optional extra but involves some carrying down steps) with the pretty Bowling canal basin between the two. An excellent family run for those wanting to sample the sights of the north bank of the Clyde.

S Pick up the cycle path at the access point in the Mountblow/ Dalmuir area (see map). Go **R** onto the path on the far bank of the canal. The Erskine Bridge will soon come into view. Follow the canal path until meeting a small white bridge across the canal.

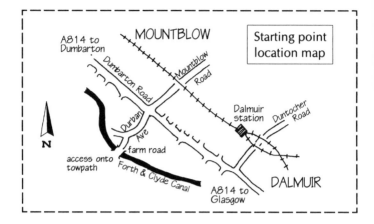

Erskine Bridge option: if you want to experience views up and down the Clyde from 180ft up in the air then you can cross and recross the bridge on opposite sides, on specially provided cycle lanes. Go **R** over the white canal bridge and cross straight over the A814 onto Barclay Street and first **L** onto Glen Road. Bear **L** into a small park area off Glen Road and continue under concrete tunnels (railway). Shortly after the water outflow point bear **L** and loop round 180 degrees uphill and find the cycle track on the left hand side of the Erskine Bridge. There are great views going both ways over the railings but beware, the view is not for those with vertigo. Don't worry if the bridge trembles under your feet when large lorries pass or in high winds; it is meant to do so to avoid breaking!

Coming to the other side of the bridge exit and carry down the second set of steps to the main road by a bridge on the right. Go **R** to cross under the bridge and just underneath go **R** up the track ¶ *Erskine Bridge*, going past the car park and gift shop on the left. Cross back over and at the other end of the bridge the cycle lane ends. Follow the track round **L** 180 degrees. Follow ¶ cycletrack and bend right past the entrance to Kilpatrick station on the left. Carry down the next steps on the left to the road and **L** onto it to a T-junction with the main road. Go **L** again here taking you back under the bridge and picking up the white bridge over the canal shortly on the **R**, and **R** over the bridge onto the cycle track.

Simply follow the cycle track and meet the lock gates on the canal just in front of two bridges over it. Take the first small bridge over the canal (straight on under the second much larger iron bridge takes you to Bowling canal basin itself and the old customs house). Carry on to the main road, straight over and bear **L** onto the track in a park area. Follow it to meet a gate and through the cycle entrance at the side onto a wooded section. Pass through a lovely cutting and Bowling tunnel to exit and cross over a road by a roundabout on the right.

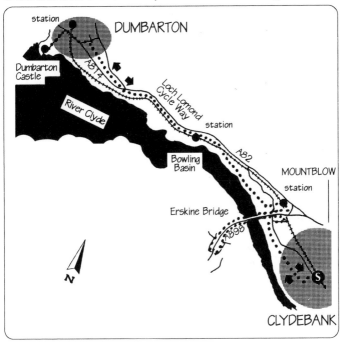

The track is now sandwiched between main road and railway and follows this course past a tourist information centre. At a T-junction with Fourth Avenue follow a ¶ **L**. Another ¶ swings you left then right back onto the cycleway itself, between houses. Under a small tunnel come to a grassy area with football pitches on the left. At the end of the grassy section go **L** down a track off the cycletrack (from this point you can see the orange railway bridge by Dumbarton East station). At the main road go **R** under that bridge and look for a **L** down Castle

Street shortly after the traffic lights. Follow to the castle at the end (entrance on the right and a lovely picnic area by the Clyde straight ahead).

You can either go back the way you came or get the train back to your starting point from the nearby Dumbarton East station.

ALONG THE WAY
• **Erskine Bridge** *Don't worry if you feel a little precarious standing on this most westerly bridge over the Clyde; it supports 30,000 tons of concrete and steel and is designed to withstand 130mph winds!*

• **Bowling Basin** *represents the western terminal locks of the Forth & Clyde Canal. Through the park after Bowling you join the course of the old Caledonian & Dumbartonshire Railway which, after 1850, took many from Glasgow to see the shores of Loch Lomond for the first time.*

•**Dumbarton Castle** *An unusual geological feature, historic monument and natural viewpoint from which to picnic whilst enjoying the Clyde spread out before you, are all uniquely combined when you terminate the route here. Entry to the castle is rewarded by a good climb to the cliff top flagpole and excellent views. Similar in origin to Stirling and Edinburgh castles, the ancient volcanic plug on which the castle is founded rises slightly incongruously in front of a more modern industrial sector of Dumbarton immediately behind it.*

Used first by Britons in the 5th century AD during the kingdom of Strathclyde, the castle gained much of its strength as it was only 2km from Drumbuck (the large scarp you pass on the right coming into

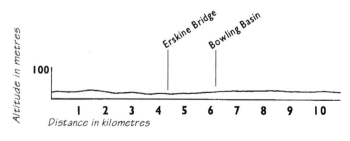

Dumbarton) to the east, then a natural fording point across the Clyde. As with numerous northern castles and aristocratic strongholds, Mary Queen of Scots was there at some time. The child queen was taken from here to the safety of France and was defeated at Langside whilst heading for that safety.

The medieval castle was largely destroyed and replaced during the 16th and 17th centuries. The addition of the Governor's House and King George's Battery after 1715 followed a failed Jacobite rebellion. In 1714 George I, a minor German prince from Hanover, had become king of England at the will of Parliament and established a Protestant succession. A Jacobite threat supporting a rival Catholic claimant to the throne ('the Pretender', the son of James II), disintegrated in Scotland but made the government wary enough to consolidate such fortifications. Although the Protestant succession was finally guaranteed under Robert Walpole, our first 'Prime Minister' during his 21 year governorship, it seemed at the time the country could fall on either side of the great Protestant/Catholic religious schism, or indeed be torn apart by it.

Alternatively if you're not interested in history you can lounge around in the grassy area between the rock and the Clyde but you would miss a great view from the top of the volcanic plug.
Open: April-Sept 0930-1900 (Sunday 1400-1900); October-March 0930-1600 (Sunday 1400-1600). Closed Thursday afternoons and all day Friday.

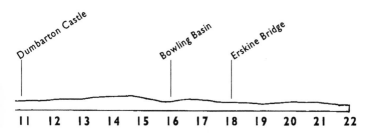

15

LOCH LOMOND

START Balloch   **Grid ref.** 395820

DISTANCE 27km/17 miles   **TIME ALLOWED** 4/5 hours

GRADIENT DIFFICULTY 2

TRACK SURFACE Mainly minor roads finishing on the Glasgow-Loch Lomond Cycleway. Some small linking sections on 'A' road.

ORDNANCE SURVEY MAPS
Unfortunately the route is split between 4 Landrangers!
64, Glasgow; 56, Loch Lomond;
57, Stirling & the Trossachs; 63, Firth of Clyde.
Most of the route is covered on 56 and 57.

ACCESS Start by the tourist information office in the town centre. Balloch itself straddles the southern end of Loch Lomond where the River Leven exits to wend its way south to the Firth of Clyde. Simply follow the A82 out of Dumbarton through Alexandria. **Car** Plenty of space in the car park by the tourist information centre. **Train** Balloch is the ultimate station on a spur off the Drumgelloch-Helensburgh line.

SUMMARY
Balloch and the southern end of Loch Lomond may seem full of tourist crowds in midsummer but if you take the trouble to explore some of the minor roads in the gently undulating hills to the east, you will find new vistas of the loch itself and the chance to visit Balloch Country Park and its fine grounds. Return to Balloch on the riverside Sustrans route, under bridges, past moored pleasure craft of all shapes and sizes. Some of the minor road section follows part of the road section of the Glasgow-Loch Lomond-Killin Cycleway.

S From the tourist information office head **L** eastwards. Just before the T-junction with the A811 take a **L** up Mollanbowie Road ¶ *Balloch Country Park*. As the road swings left go **R** opposite the entrance to Balloch Castle Country Park (worth a look - see page 80). Follow this road to a T-junction and go **L**. Almost straight away pick up a minor **R** by the Ballochmyle Hotel. After a twisting climb the road levels and straightens to a **L** ¶ *Gartocharn* (look out for the distinctive rocky spur of Duncryne ahead to your right). Descend through houses at the back of Gartocharn to meet the A811.

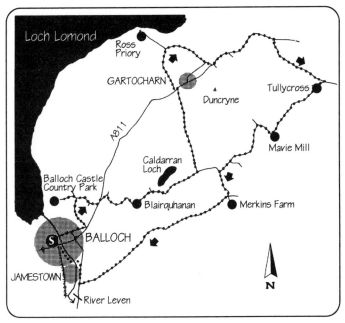

Go **L** then **R** off the main road down Ross Loan just over the bridge. This minor road loops round 180 degrees past Ross Priory at the most northerly part of this loop, with several good vantage points over the loch and the hills that huddle up to its shores. Go **L** on meeting the main road again and in just under a couple of kilometres take the second minor **R** (easy to miss); you know you are correct here if the road leads to a single house on the right, on a left hand bend. Wind through wooded countryside to the hamlet of Tullycross and go **R** in the middle of the buildings.

Bending through Mavie Mill take the next **L** ¶ *Caldarvan station* to a T-junction (don't look for the station on the map - the actual service was closed down in the 1930's!) and go **L** again ¶ *Jamestown and Caldarvan*. At the next junction opposite Merkins farm go **R** and drop to the main road. Go **R** at the main road. As the church comes into view pick up the path **L** opposite the right ¶ *Jamestown Industrial Estate*. Just over the bridge descend the steps and bear left onto the cycleway, keeping the Leven on your right. This small last stretch takes you past a marina and Loch Lomond Rowing Club. The start in Balloch is under the second bridge and up to the **L**.

ALONG THE WAY

• **Balloch** has boat tours of many of the islands and places of interest on Loch Lomond, although one of the most famous passenger steamers that sailed the loch in the 1950's, the Maid of the Loch, is the subject of a funding attempt to restore it. In times when foreign holidays were virtually unheard of for most, Balloch was crowded with the working classes from Glasgow enjoying their spare time. Ponder at close hand the attractions of Inchmurrin ('grassy island'), with its castle and deer park, and Inchcailloch ('women's island'), with its cemetery and Rob Roy associations.

• **Balloch Castle** was home to the powerful Lennox family before they moved to the island of Inchmurrin for greater safety. The ancient castle is long gone but a more modern one is worth a visit, and the grounds offer superb views of Loch Lomond. Set in 200 acres of beautiful parkland it was constructed in the early nineteenth century for a Glasgow financier. There is a fairy glen and it's possible to see Cameron House, one time residence of the novelist Tobias Smollet.

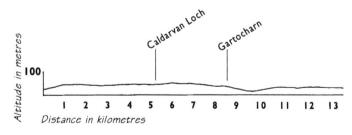

• **Loch Lomond** was formed over 10,000 years ago by the action of a huge glacier moving south. It is Britain's biggest stretch of inland waterway at 27½ square miles. The Highland Boundary Line, a huge geological fault line, runs directly across the loch marked by the islands of Inchmurrin, Torrinch, Creinch and Inchcailloch. In human terms the area was one of profound conflict of attitude and lifestyles in the eighteenth century, as clan highlanders robbed and extorted from the farmers who rented land at the foot of the loch. Pick up any leaflet and you can't fail to miss the modern day commercial appeal to the tourist trade of one of the most famous robbers of all, Rob Roy.

The surrounding area has a rich and diverse natural habitat; over 200 bird species and 25% of Britain's wild plants have been recorded in the area. Because of the outstanding natural beauty of the area it was proposed for National Park status in 1947 when these designations came into being, with their credo of balancing leisure and local interests with the beauty of the land. It did not achieve this but in 1988 became part of Loch Lomond Regional Park. There is much debate about to what extent designation as the former, with its associated financial assistance and regional controls, would have really protected the area from the pressures of mass tourism. In some of the 'flashpoints' around the loch in summer this pressure is especially noticeable - 40,000 people may visit the loch on a good summer day.

Try to pick out Ben Lomond from a suitable viewpoint on the route (for example the one in Balloch Castle grounds). It lies on the north eastern shore and at 974m is Scotland's most southerly Munro (mountain over 3000ft or 914m).

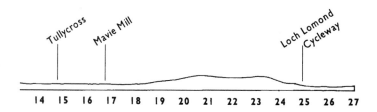

16

STRATHCLYDE COUNTRY PARK

START *Strathclyde Country Park*   **Grid ref.** *722583*

DISTANCE *13km/8 miles*   **TIME ALLOWED** *2 hours*

GRADIENT DIFFICULTY *A fairly tricky 2 on the South Calder Water section, otherwise a very easy 1*

TRACK SURFACE *Some road within the park where it may be busy at peak hours, but traffic is restricted to 15mph. Otherwise tarmac paths and some hardpacked earth surface by the South Calder Water.*

ORDNANCE SURVEY MAP *Landranger 64, Glasgow*
Information leaflets about the park at the visitor centre

ACCESS *Enter the country park from junction 5 of the M74.* **Car** *After passing signs within the park for camp & caravan site, visitor centre and Bothwellhaugh Pavilion, use the first car park on the left.* **Train** *Airbles station in south Motherwell is 5 minutes' ride from the park.*

SUMMARY

This route has two distinct parts. The 4km/2½ miles or so up and down the South Calder Water is a beautiful natural environment taking you under the impressive Orbiston Viaduct. Whilst the track surface itself is reasonably hardpacked there are a number of short and steep ups and downs; it may not be suitable for younger children as there is a drop to the river on the outward leg. Always remain under control on this section and be aware pedestrians also explore the same route.

The rest of the route is ideal, with excellent and generally flat surfaces for family cycling and all types of bikes. Indeed there are no restrictions on cycling anywhere within the park so feel free to explore at your leisure (this selected route covers my own favourite spots).

S Commence by continuing on the road away from junction 5 and shortly after the fun fair and roundabout come to a road bridge over the South Calder Water. Just before the bridge look for a smaller track to the **L** into woods. Just before entering woods cross over a small crossroads of tracks (right here takes you down to an old packhorse bridge known as the Roman Bridge - worth a look but the path after the bridge becomes unsuitable for bikes).

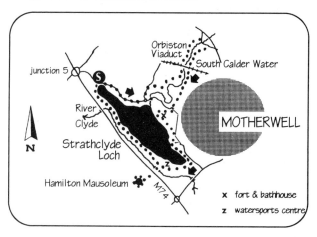

After a climb through woods you reach a split. Go **R** towards a play area and **R** at the T-junction near here. At the next immediate fork go **L** to come alongside the golf course on your left. At the first split go **R** which drops away downhill to an open grass area. Follow the lone path on the left of this area and into the trees to run alongside the river on your right as the path narrows. Keeping on this 'roller coaster' path pass under the towering Orbiston Viaduct and past a weir below you on the right. As the woods disappear the track bears left of a disused road bridge. On meeting the road go **R** over the bridge, and ignoring a minor path on the right pick up the second wider **R.**

Stay on the main track past the weir on the right and push up a small set of steps. At a minor crossroads go **R** to another push up more steps. Stay on the main track to pass back under the viaduct. You now skirt a north Motherwell housing estate on the left and bearing right at every opportunity here pass a football pitch on the left. Pick up the downhill tarmac run to a road and cross over to the horseshoe sign on the other side and go **R.**

After the car park on the right bear **L** at the road bridge to the Roman Bathhouse on the left. Bear **R** at all junctions (except an acute back right by the edge of the loch). Skirt in front of a picnic area and car park following the south eastern end of the loch and to the road. Go **R** here onto the road going past the water sports centre on the right. Shortly after this go **L** over the bridge ¶ *mausoleum*. Crossing the Clyde and passing under the M74, follow the main track to the mausoleum on the right. Dismount and have a stroll around. Return to the lochside road on the same route under the M74 and over the Clyde.

Go **L** onto the road and skirt the edge of the loch to its end, crossing a road to take you back to the car park starting point.

ALONG THE WAY

• **Strathclyde Country Park** *itself combines a host of outdoor activities; camping site, watersports (with equipment for hire) and many other sports facilities, with a funfair and the opportunity to take it all in by bike! Cafe available at the water sports centre.*

• **The Orbiston Viaduct** *towers above you on your ride up the left bank of the South Calder Water. It houses the west coast railway line down to England. The sandstone cliff area just before this was the site of a failed attempt in the 1820's to set up a co-operative community along the lines of that at New Lanark, founded by Robert Owen.*

• **Bothwellhaugh Fort and Bathhouse** *lay on a communication line south from the Antonine Wall. Its remains can be observed on the route as you meet the South Calder Water, just before it feeds into Strathclyde Loch. The original site of the bathhouse was submerged when the water in the artificial Strathclyde Loch reached its full*

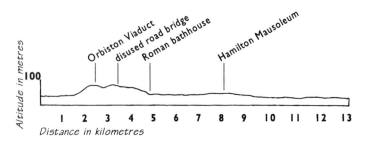

84

height, but the remains you see here were excavated and reconstructed above water level on a specially made platform. The bathhouse was more akin to the modern sauna, containing a number of rooms ranging from unheated through tepid to hot.

• **Hamilton Mausoleum** When completed in the mid-nineteenth century this decorous and imposing building cost around £30,000, a quite immense sum at the time. It was built by the 10th Duke of Hamilton for himself, though he in fact died before its completion. His body was later transferred to the family burial ground. So rather than a glorious monument to aristocratic glory, the building seems more of a beautiful, classically designed folly. The duke's palace itself was destroyed because of subsidence. There are guided tours of the interior, enabling you to sample the strange acoustics and equally incredible crypt, chapel and original bronze doors, amongst other features.

Hamilton
Mausoleum

In Clachan of Campsie (Route 2)

LENNOXTOWN FOREST

START *Cadder Village*   **Grid ref.** *615724*

DISTANCE *19km/12 miles*   **TIME ALLOWED** *3 hours*

GRADIENT DIFFICULTY *2, with some grade 3 in the forest*

TRACK SURFACE *Off-road rights of way generally of good quality but may be muddy in places. Forestry Commission tracks hardpacked with one very narrow uphill section. Some quiet minor country roads.*

ORDNANCE SURVEY MAP *Landranger 64, Glasgow*

ACCESS *Start in the old part of Cadder by the church, north of a small bridge over the Forth & Clyde Canal. Heading north from Bishopbriggs on the A803 look for Cadder Road on the left (if you reach the roundabout by the retail park you have gone too far). Follow the road to the bridge.* **Car** *No car park in the vicinity but look for off road parking after turning down Cadder Road.* **Train** *The start is 3km north up the A803 from Bishopbriggs station.*

SUMMARY
Definitely one for mountain bikes. An easy start over a golf course and over the River Kelvin belies steeper climbs towards Lennoxtown Wood and once in the woods you make use of narrow and tricky tracks for mountain bikers wanting a challenge. Be prepared for several lifts over gates or fences.

Once in the woods you are on Forestry Commission land, so you can short cut using tracks marked on your map which are wider and easier than the difficult smaller tracks north of the woods, if you wish. In any case, take a compass into the woods as there are few viewpoints and numerous mazey paths. The scarp face beneath Lairs towers to the north of the FC woods, whilst the road to the east of the forest yields great views over numerous towns on the flatter plain to the south.

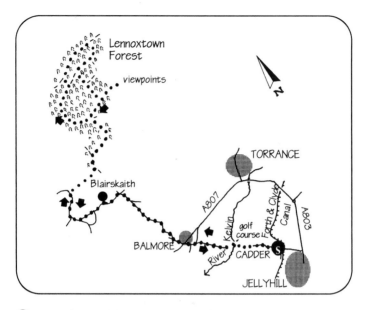

S Over the canal bridge at the end of Cadder Road turn **R** (not the road straight on ¶ *golf club*). Almost immediately the road splits; bear **L** past the church on the left and through the gates ahead. Past houses at the end of the vehicle track follow straight on as the track narrows. Following past the golf course on the right the track becomes a little muddy at the bridge (give way to pedestrians on narrow sections) then widens out after crossing to lead you to a T-junction at the back of the village of Balmore. Go **L** here to another T-junction with the A807.

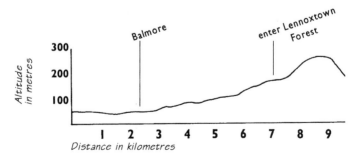

Go more or less straight over here up Glenorchard Road past the church hall on the right. Remain on the same road bending right at the next junction (ignoring Golf Course Road on the left). Follow the pleasant country road for just over a kilometre to a crossroads and go **L**. Pass the next left ¶ *Baldernock Primary School*. Shortly after this take the next minor **R** and a steep climb brings you to a hardpacked vehicle track on the **R** between boulders, pleasantly tree lined with views to the right over northern Glasgow. Follow the track to a T-junction and go **L** to go over a fence stile (carry). Pick up the line of the grass track through rough grassland. Ignore a minor left as the main track takes you to a gate at the edge of Forestry Commission woods.

Go over the stile and climb a difficult track to a T-junction on a bend and go **L**. At the next T-junction go **L** again. Ignore a minor forking track to the left. Go **L** at the next fork giving a great view of the scarp in front of Lairs. Bear right and downhill and **R** at the next fork onto a very narrow path with overhanging trees. A small blue ringed waymarker confirms you are on the right track as does an old wall on the left. At the bottom of the drop fork **R** and bend round right to a very steep climb.

After this very hard, technical climb meet the main track again at a T-junction with a bend and go **L**. Follow the main track past a minor left and straight on to exit at the tarmac road at the end where the mast faces you. You have the option of riding on to the left for a short while, for great views of the flatter lands to the south (double back on yourself at a good viewpoint as there is no easy return route in this direction). To return go **R** at the 'mast' junction to lead down a forest track to your entry point on the **L** at the next junction. After taking this left retrace outward steps.

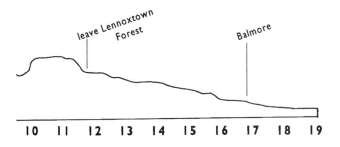

QUEENSIDE MUIR

START *Lochwinnoch*   **Grid ref.** *356590*

DISTANCE *20km/12½ miles*   **TIME ALLOWED** *3½ hours*

GRADIENT DIFFICULTY *A long, and in places hard, grade 2, followed by a freewheeling downhill return of equal length*

TRACK SURFACE *Initial single track minor road gives way to good hardpacked but stony vehicle track*

ORDNANCE SURVEY MAP
Landranger 63, Firth of Clyde

ACCESS   *Lochwinnoch village is about 17km south of Port Glasgow by the side of Castle Semple Loch, on the south eastern edge of the Clyde Muirshiel Regional Park. Start by the Castle Semple visitor centre, at the side of the loch (well signed).* **Car** *Free parking by the visitor centre.* **Train** *Lochwinnoch station is only a few minutes' ride away on the southern side of the loch.*

SUMMARY
Initially the road section climbs by the friendly, idyllic wooded upper banks of the River Calder, but do not be deceived! The countryside opens out to wide, rolling moorland reminiscent of a Yorkshire Dales landscape. Joining the gravel road after the Muirshiel Country Park visitor centre will add to the difficulty after initial steep road stages. The climb is worth it as the moorland opens out in front of you; an unusual landscape for central Scotland. However you still need a fair amount of stamina as you climb from near sea level at Castle Semple Loch to around 350m (1150ft) to terminate the almost continuous uphill at disused mines, and return on a glorious downhill sweep back to the valley. Mountain bike recommended for the track section; a possible lift over a locked gate onto this track.

S Exit **R** from the car park and under the old railway bridge that now carries the Sustrans route, to meet the B786 running through the centre of Lochwinnoch. Go **L** through the shops to the first crossroads and go **R** up Calder Street. This road narrows to follow the side of the river for a short while, past an attractive weir. Some small hard climbs bring you to a T-junction with the 'B' road, going **L** and immediate **L** ¶ *Muirshiel Country Park*, back onto a minor road.

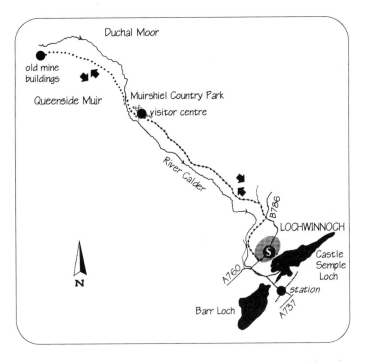

This road climbs up the side of the narrowing valley on the left as the country gradually opens to moorland. Follow it up, ignoring any splits off to the right through woods or smaller paths. Reach the visitor centre on the left and carry on the main road following it to a gate and possible lift over it onto the hardpacked road. It's then about a 5km climb to the disused mines. Shortly after the gate cross over the second modern bridge (the first is a disused wreck and not easy for bikes). Carry on ascending to the **R** immediately after the bridge.

After recharging your batteries at the mines it's all easy going to follow the route you took out back to Castle Semple Loch; be careful to be under control at all times on the long downhill stretches.

ALONG THE WAY

• **Castle Semple Loch** visitor centre sits by the Paisley to Irvine cycle route and is a popular spot for water sports (with hire facilities) and general relaxation by the waterside.

• **Muirshiel Country Park** is part of the Clyde Muirshiel Regional Park that covers 102 square miles of beautifully varied countryside, roughly defined by Greenock, Inverkip, Largs and Lochwinnoch at its edges. A huge variety of plants and animals can be found in the small area (details at the visitor centre). Red grouse, curlew and skylark are hunted on the open moor by a number of birds of prey. Muirshiel Country Park consists of the policy woodland and former Muirshiel estate.

• **The Barytes Mine** at the end of the road mined this mineral up until 1969 and indeed, the road you have ascended on is made largely of this mineral, used as a pigment in such everyday products as toothpaste and paper. From the mines you can look north over Duchal Moor where lies an unusual miniature railway used for transportation of grouse shooters.

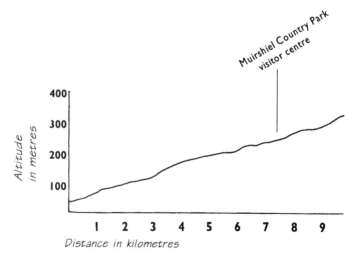

Looking down the Calder Valley, Muirshiel Country Park

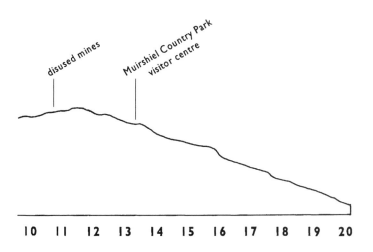

disused mines

Muirshiel Country Park
visitor centre

10 11 12 13 14 15 16 17 18 19 20

HILLSIDE GUIDES

■ *Circular Walks - Yorkshire Dales*

WHARFEDALE
THREE PEAKS
WENSLEYDALE
SWALEDALE
HOWGILL FELLS
NIDDERDALE
MALHAMDALE

■ *Circular Walks - North York Moors*

WESTERN MOORS
SOUTHERN MOORS
NORTHERN MOORS

■ *Circular Walks - South Pennines*

BRONTE COUNTRY
CALDERDALE
ILKLEY MOOR

■ *Circular Walks - Lancashire*

BOWLAND
PENDLE & the RIBBLE

■ *Circular Walks - North Pennines*

TEESDALE
EDEN VALLEY

■ **WALKING COUNTRY TRIVIA QUIZ** ■
Over 1000 questions on the great outdoors

ACROSS THE NORTH

■ *Long Distance Walks*

THE COAST TO COAST WALK
DALES WAY COMPANION
CLEVELAND WAY COMPANION
FURNESS WAY
WESTMORLAND WAY
CUMBERLAND WAY
NORTH BOWLAND TRAVERSE (David Johnson)
LADY ANNE'S WAY (Sheila Gordon)

■ *Hillwalking - Lake District*

OVER LAKELAND MOUNTAINS - the 2000ft peaks
OVER LAKELAND FELLS - the sub-2000ft fells

■ *Yorkshire Pub Walks* by Valerie Yewdall

HARROGATE & the WHARFE VALLEY
HAWORTH & the AIRE VALLEY

■ *BIKING COUNTRY* by Richard Peace

YORKSHIRE DALES CYCLE WAY
WEST YORKSHIRE CYCLE WAY
MOUNTAIN BIKING - WEST & SOUTH YORKSHIRE
GLASGOW Clyde Valley & Loch Lomond

■ *POCKET BIKING GUIDES* by Paul Hannon

AIRE VALLEY   **CALDERDALE**

■ *Large format colour hardback* ■

FREEDOM OF THE DALES
Exploring the Yorkshire Dales on Foot

LOG OF THE RIDES

RIDE	DATE	NOTES
1		
2		
3		
4		
5		
6		
7		
8		
9		
10		
11		
12		
13		
14		
15		
16		
17		
18		